Life IS LIKE CLIMBING A MOUNTAIN

DR. JAMES E. BRUCE

"Your story is our priority"

LitPrime Solutions
21250 Hawthorne Blvd
Suite 500, Torrance, CA 90503
www.litprime.com
Phone: 1-800-981-9893

Published by LitPrime Solutions: 10/31/2023

ISBN: 979-8-88703-305-1(sc)
ISBN: 979-8-88703-306-8(hc)
ISBN: 979-8-88703-307-5(e)

Library of Congress Control Number: 2023918921

Contents

A motivational, inspirational and a spiritual tool that will guide the reader towards accomplishing a literal climb of an actual mountain, or a virtual climb that might take the form of realizing a goal, dream or aspiration.

By James E. Bruce Sr., Ph.D.

Preface

Can you remember the last time someone sarcastically told you to "take a hike"? Perhaps you were offended and, if so, good for you, and more power to them. You received only what you've allowed. Actually, you have empowered that person by granting them control over your feelings and emotions. No doubt that person intended to be insulting to you. Obviously, their order to you was maybe hurtful because you have not yet read this book. Of course, you could not have read this book since it was not written. Okay, let us let the past be the past. But from this point forward, if someone thinks that they can offend you by telling you to "take a hike", just tell them thank you, and that you are engaged in one right now or you were just thinking about one. You can inform them that "taking a hike" is a high level exploration whereby you are exercising your virtual mountain climbing skills. So, you will no longer be offended by an order to "take a hike", but instead, you will be encouraged to explore, believe, and achieve.

During and after your virtual mountain climbing excursion, you will be prompted to assess your personal character qualities during and after having emerged through the virtual mountain climb venture.

Before beginning your journey, you must recite and believe these most powerful words: I can, I will, and it will happen.

The objective of this book is to inform, educate, inspire, and motivate individuals and groups toward understanding oneself and others through a literal or virtual mountain climbing experience. The aim is to introduce the reader to a literary journey that involves the process and the act of mountain climbing. This book brings recognition to literal mountains that could be comprised of rocks, trees, ice, snow, and dirt. A mountain could be made up of a combination of the five kinds just listed. A volcanic mountain should be added, as a living rock, to this list of literal mountains. The volatility inherent in a volcanic mountain parallels the vulnerability and the potential explosiveness that exists in the individual human experience, as well as within our local and world communities.

These literal or physical mountains are used as a metaphor to offer insight towards understanding the dynamics and the challenges that are involved in the process of climbing a virtual mountain. The mountain climbing process might become more meaningful to an explorer who may climb a virtual mountain that might ultimately take the form of realizing a goal, dream, or aspiration.

This book explores the spiritual aspect of the physical mountain, particularly how the physical mountain has been a reference place for some people who testify to having a life-changing experience.

Finally, this book provides a strategic working roadmap that will transform the reader into a dreamer, and then into an explorer, a believer, and finally, an achiever. The achiever, in retrospect, will be inspired to recall and then recite the most powerful words: I said I can, I know that I would, and I made it happen.

This mountain climbing model is useful towards attaining individual, personal or collective goals, set in areas such as education, business, wealth building, job or career development, marriage, political aspirations, geographical relocating, re-establishing oneself, raising children, leading or managing sports teams, hiring and managing a work force, or even for the military that strategizes to win wars.

This "climbing a mountain model" can be used for creating a strategic map towards achieving other personal goals, such as writing a book, building a house from the ground up, or regaining physical or mental health. Similarly, for organizations, this "climbing a mountain model" can be used as a guide when setting an organization's growth plans in motion. The principles are the same.

The First Dedication

To start off, this book is designed to be a little different from other books. For instance, usually a book will not have more than one distinct dedication, but this book does. In fact, this book has two dedications. So the dedications are distinguished as the first dedication and the second dedication. Hmmm, I know that's different. That's right; I said it would be different.

This book is dedicated firstly to The Almighty God which made heaven and earth, the seas and all that in them is. The honor is due Him because my help came from Him. God blessed me to understand that He is a Spirit and that I must worship Him in Spirit and in Truth. The earth is the Lord's and the fullness thereof, and they that dwell therein. I also understand that everything He made was good. The mountain, unlike everything else that God ordained, has a special relationship to humans and other living organisms. The mountain is a unique natural resource that can provide the basic necessities of life, such as food and shelter, for humans, animals, birds and insects. The mountain embodies other natural resources such as trees, rocks, soil, streams and pure water for drinking. The co-existence of the vast variety of natural resources that are encamped within the mountain intrigues me because I envision these component parts that make up the mountain as a community within the universe that, for the moment, could be called a mountain.

I am humbled for the spiritual wisdom and understanding that has been revealed to me concerning mountains and the human spirit that can be understood for its relationship to a literal mountain and a mountain climbing experience. This book has recognized a literal mountain as a metaphor to bring understanding to the virtual and spiritual mountains that humans desire and sometimes are forced to climb. For some people, the thought or invitation to climb a literal mountain is out of the question. Consciously and unconsciously humans climb virtual or spiritual mountains all the time. However, some people will make a virtual or spiritual mountain climb in one day, while others will take a lifetime. If a lifetime is what it takes, that's fine, as long as the explorer is able to answer the question: "what is your mountain?"

Again, this book is firstly dedicated to The Almighty God for guiding me and directing my path as I journeyed to write and complete this book. Throughout the process, I was faithful and acknowledged Him. The fruits of our relationship have allowed me to finish this book. I am now satisfied that I have successfully climbed my virtual mountain.

The Second Dedication

The declaration of the second dedication of this book is made to my amazing wife, Sylvia, my fantastic three young- adult children, particularly my youngest son Semaj, who, at the age of eleven, daringly and bravely journeyed with me on a literal mountain climb in 2006.

To Ray Washington, and Alan Jacobson. I find it ironic to be dedicating a book to you since you personify and embody the meaning and essence of dedication. You have been dedicated and loyal to a friendship/brotherhood for many years. You have always been there for my family and me, even when it came to finishing this book. Your friendship and support have made my virtual mountain climbs a breeze. Thank you.

Additionally, I honor my mother, Louise, and all my past ancestors who have successfully climbed hundreds, or perhaps thousands of virtual mountains in their lives, and have been to the mountain top, and have seen the promise land. I dedicate this book to you.

This book is dedicated to my good friend, avid mountain climber extraordinaire, Chuck Peters. Chuck, this book is in part dedicated to you, hopefully to inspire and then motivate you to write the much needed book about mountain climbing that I've been talking to you about for years. You need to let the world know about the hundreds of literal mountains you've climbed. I will save a big thank you for the acknowledgement section of this learning tool. Chuck, go ahead and claim your virtual mountain.

Speaking of learning tools, and while I am still dedicating this book, this book is also dedicated to all the eventual millions of readers, who I will call explorers, believers, and then achievers. My hope is that you will become inspired and motivated and will venture a virtual or spiritual mountain climb. I hope that you will select a virtual mountain to climb and apply the strategy that I offer in this learning tool. As you read and learn from this book, I trust that you will understand the literal mountain metaphor and be able to recognize the parallel of how life is like climbing a mountain. I know that you will have a life-changing experience.

And finally, this book is dedicated to all the positive people who encouraged me to take this literary journey. I want to also acknowledge the few people who showed very little interest as I climbed this virtual mountain. Both groups of people have inspired me in ways they would not understand. For instance, the positive people pulled me along, and the negative people pushed me along. Again, the book is dedicated to you because with your input, I reached the summit.

When occasions arise, and thank you expressions are in order, when people are to be recognized by name, almost always, a name or two is omitted. Just so that will not happen here, I will provide a blank line so that if you feel you are deserving of a name mention, by all means, insert your name on the line: _____ .

Acknowledgements

The grateful spirit of this work acknowledges the wisdom and understanding of the message that is presented in this book. The deeper message is more profound than the familiar cliché: *Life is like climbing a mountain.* This book is intended to serve as a motivational, inspirational, and spiritual guide that is grounded in one's faith as the substance of things hoped for and the evidence of things not seen.

I want to acknowledge in advance the hope for a life-changing or spiritual transformation that should occur as a result of the reader's interest, understanding and application of the virtual and spiritual mountain climbing methodologies. The virtual mountain climbing written exercise found in the latter part of this book is designed to serve as a strategic road map that should invigorate the reader/explorer to an energy level that should drive the explorer with confidence to profess that: I can and I will.

In the like spirit, I want to acknowledge, and give a big thanks to my friend of more than twenty years, an avid mountain climber extraordinaire, ladies and gentlemen: Mr. Chuck Peters. Now, I get the chance to officially thank you for agreeing to take my youngest and daring son Semaj and me on that early morning literal mountain climb. I told you, and you understood that I needed to make that actual mountain climb, so that I could speak from experience and finish this book. With your help, I was able to coach the reader/ explorer through an actual mountain climb. Of course, some finer details might be missing, but I guess that is where you would come in with your book that I've been encouraging you to write… so get busy.

A great big thank you goes to Mr. Ray Washington, another true friend for more than twenty years. Ray, you are the epitome of a real friend. You are better than a brother. I feel like Moses, so, you must be Aaron. Thank you for the first editing; you helped me to convey the message and the wisdom. I must recognize Patricia McPherson who spent much time final editing, revising, and proofreading to make the book the best language it could be. Thank you Patty.

Lastly, I want thank and acknowledge the many people who encouraged me to hurry up and get this book done because they want to get their personal copy. So, here it is.

Life Is Like Climbing a Mountain
By James Bruce Sr., Ph.D.

Introduction

This book begins by asking a two-part question; what are mountains and what are mountains used for? Of course, there are many kinds of mountains, and mountains have many uses and functions. We shall address this two-part question in reverse. A quick answer, although partial, to the latter part of the question might provide that a mountain is to be climbed and explored. Now, in response to the former part of the question as to what a mountain is, similarly, a quick answer would be: It depends on the type of mountain that you reference; there are physical or literal mountains and there are figurative or virtual mountains.

This book is written to serve as a motivational, inspirational, and a spiritual tool that will guide the reader towards accomplishing a literal climb of an actual mountain, and a virtual climb that may take the form of realizing a personal realization or awareness, goal, dream, or aspiration. The reader of this book will begin as just that, *the reader*. As the reader progresses through this journey, a new title will be bestowed; that of, *a dreamer*. As the dream becomes more vivid, the dreamer becomes a *believer*. As the believer ascends the mountain, the believer will become *an explorer*. Ultimately, the explorer will become *an achiever* of a desired goal or a summit, only to realize the power and potential in the actions manifested in the words, I CAN. The words, I CAN, I WILL, and IT WILL HAPPEN, will be the prelude to a new path and yet another journey. Yes, the explorer will investigate and pursue new plateaus backdropped by the new horizons of the literal or virtual mountain.

A virtual mountain can also be described as a spiritual "overcome" or breakthrough experience. This book includes a discussion and explanation of a spiritual mountain, presented in figurative or virtual context, within the spiritual realm. A creative aspect of this book is that the author identifies the various compositions of literal mountains such as rock, ice, snow, trees, dirt either in whole or in some combined form. These mountains are presented and then discussed in the context of a virtual climb. This book both recognizes and highlights the source and force of a volcanic mountain. A volcanic mountain discussion will articulate how the effects of a literal volcanic eruption can be perceived as positive and negative at the same time. A similar analysis is noted within humans who sometime explode with emotions when tempted, bombarded and pressured internally, externally or both simultaneously. Finally, a point of view is revealed that, like the volcano, the eruptions or changes we ourselves or others see within us are merely the end result of changes that have often occurred unnoticed either within us or our environment long ago.

The intent behind a mountain climb venture is to experience a transformation. For some people a mountain climb experience produces an effect that invariably changes one's self-confidence; at a minimum, the experience places a new lens and view on one's horizon. The new attitude becomes a testament of one's faith and inner strength which demonstrates a spirit that says about climbing a literal, figurative or spiritual mountain, "I CAN", "I WILL", and eventually, "I DID!"

This book concludes with a tested written exercise that offers a strategic working plan or roadmap to ensure and encourage positive personal or organizational transformation. The exercise, when completed, is guaranteed to produce an opportunity for the reader/adventurer to consider a new attitude and perspective about life and its many challenges. The exercise will certainly introduce life realities that parallel a literal mountain climb, but presented within the framework of a figurative or virtual mountain climb. Some aspects of change for individuals or organizations to be realized include, but are not limited to, attitude, methodology or approach to performing particular functions, critical thinking and analysis, expanded purview and capacity building.

This exercise will essentially provide a roadmap for the reader to follow as a sure plan of success in identifying, defining, preparing, and then ultimately climbing a virtual mountain -- that series of mountains that are inherently implanted within the physical and spiritual experience we call life.

Chapter One

Understanding the Mountain

Physical or literal mountains are universal and often present a very breathtaking sight to behold. Physical or literal mountains come in a variety of forms and sizes. For instance, depending on what part of the world it is situated, a mountain could be comprised of rocks, trees, ice, snow, or dirt, either singularly or in any combination. Also, depending on its physical location, the physical characteristics of a mountain can change, sometimes dramatically, given the season, climate, altitude or other environmental, physiological or geological instance at a particular moment in time; even time itself. Additionally, there are volcanic mountains. Volcanic mountains are made up mainly of rock, albeit volcanic rock. Volcanic mountains have a special characteristic quite different from other mountains, and should be included in a discussion to understand the dynamics and the challenges involved with successfully exploring physical mountains.

Unlike other mountains, the volcanic mountain is a type of 'living mountain'. Since volcanic mountains are more unique than the other five kinds of mountains, and are subject to drastic changes, and often volatile, a separate section is devoted in this book to speak about the volcanic mountain as a metaphor to the human life and spirit. As a metaphor, the volcanic mountain is highlighted in this discussion of mountains in order to bring recognition to its volatility and power. The characteristics of the volcanic mountain are acknowledged as significant towards understanding how the living aspects of volcanic mountains are similar to the individual human life experience as well as towards understanding the constant changes that occur within society.

Certain parallels can be drawn between the nature of the volcanic mountain and that of the basic human and how, in very similar ways, both present products and by-products that impact surrounding and distant environments. An erupting volcanic mountain generates, maintains, and at some point releases a product, called lava, which has the capacity to impact the surrounding environment. Oftentimes, the impact has a destructive effect. Contrary, however, to this is the lava's ability to form new areas of land that can nourish and sustain new life. Similarly, humans have the capacity to generate, maintain, and at some point release with great force a product that has the ability to impact destructively within one's surrounding environment. That product may be recognized as anger, aggression, or violence. Contrary, however, to a human's ability in certain controlled circumstances, to form, nourish and sustain renewed passions for survival, determination, drive, power, ambition, endurance, perseverance and the will to succeed. These passions likewise fuel the need to summon great internal and/or physical strengths to perform otherwise impossible feats: lifting a heavy object to free an injured or trapped person, jump in to fend off an attacker or attacking animal, risking one's life to rush into a burning building to rescue a child, devising a complex solution or completing a complex, time-sensitive task when everyone says it can not be done or expects you to fail. Just as the intense heat of exploding lava and huge plumes of smoke and ash can have an physiological, emotional, and environmental impact hundreds of miles from the volcano, so, too, can the positive and negative by-products of human aggression or anger have an impact on the land, environment, and any and all forms of life that inhabit this planet.

Though the volcanic 'living' mountain, like humans, possess energy that can manifest in a negative or positive way, unlike the mountain, humans for the greater part, possess the cognitive, decision-making faculties to determine if, when, where, why and what positive or negative energies will be released as a result of pressure build-up.

A physical or literal mountain climb can be spiritually influenced. A literal mountain climb can bring a person into a spiritual transformation that could display an insightful revelation of a new vision, a dream, a prophecy, or an epiphany. Typically physical mountains become the stages or platforms to receive spiritual power that initiates a life- changing experience.

A spiritual transformation usually takes shape from within, and will have a profound impact on one's sense of purpose. Often the purpose is demonstrated by the acknowledgement of a message and a plan to inform, lead or guide others -- more often than not, masses of people -- to another spiritual or social plateau.

A figurative or virtual mountain, on the other hand, can result in a physical manifestation of a desire, dream, mission, goal or aspiration. A figurative or virtual mountain climb occurrence seems to hinge on one's faith, which is the substance of things hoped for and the evidence of things not seen. Faith alone is not enough. Faith must be combined with works, skills, tools, support systems, and personal determination that will solidify one's belief that "I CAN", "I WILL", and "IT WILL HAPPEN." The level of faith and personal determination is measured by one's motivation, efforts, and definition of the mountain they desire to climb. Furthermore, a person's motivation is measured by one's focus and faith. Now one's faith can be qualified as the faith in oneself, the faith in other humans, past and present, or faith in a supreme being we call God.

Ultimately, a successful virtual mountain climb begins with a thought or an idea. The thought or the idea is driven by one's desire to see the thought or the idea come to fruition. As the thought or idea begins to take on life, the active virtual mountain climb begins. This maturation process, or virtual excursion, if not aborted completely, will continue for the virtual climber, until the virtual climber has been declared an achiever; in other words, the virtual mountain climber has realized the desire, dream, mission, goal or aspiration. So, one's faith has translated one from a dreamer to a believer to an achiever. The achiever then looks to investigate, pursue, and conquer new and other virtual mountains.

The latter part of this book explores many examples and discussions of physical, spiritual, and, in some cases, virtual mountains. For instance, in biblical times and also in modern history, physical mountains have been the stages for theatrics, platforms for divine interventions, places of refuge, havens for peace, and backdrops for war. The physical mountain has been a source for gaining spiritual power and strength. It has been recognized as a site for recreation, a place where some define achievement, and a field for competitions that measure endurance and strength.

Physical and figurative mountains are referenced in practically all genres of music, poetry, national anthems, sermons and favorite political speeches, even in personal testimonies of some who have witnessed an "out of body" death experience. In the animal world, the word mountain distinguishes some species of wildlife that would otherwise not be distinguished. For instance, as opposed to a typical goat, bear or lion, a mountain goat, mountain bear or a mountain lion specifically indicates that the natural habitat of these goats, bears and lions are in the mountains.

The energies and capacities of a person's spiritual mountain climb are personal and are sometimes difficult to explain or express. Often, there might be internal or external struggles that could hinder or negatively affect one's spiritual mountain climbing experience. For instance, the internal struggle might be evident when the person who is experiencing the spiritual mountain climb questions or resists the active spiritual transformation. Similarly, other people outside of the direct experience might question, challenge, or doubt the authenticity of a claim that an active spiritual transformation is in progress, or that a spiritual change has taken place, particularly with the person who is being doubted. This point might be made clearer as some people who profess to be prophets or have the gift of prophecy are doubted or discredited, or those who claim to be visionaries are ridiculed or discounted.

The highlight of this book is to consider the virtual mountain climb practice, although the literal climb is studied and used as a metaphor to understand how life is like climbing a mountain. The last part of this book provides a strategic road map template that will guide the reader through a working plan to successfully venture and complete a literal or virtual mountain climb. For this exercise, we will call the reader an explorer, one who might desire to complete a virtual mountain climb. The reader/explorer should be declared an "achiever" when this book has been thoroughly read, and appropriate concepts have been integrated into a plan to climb a physical or virtual mountain. When a custom strategic plan has been executed, the explorer will be recognized as an achiever, once again.

The author's personal virtual mountain climb will have been deemed a success if the explorer is able to be inspired to complete the strategic roadmap, orchestrate an action plan with a lens focused on the explorer pursuing the virtual mountain, and then reaches the peak of whatever level they aspire.

Throughout the world, physical mountains have unique sizes, shapes and characteristics. After describing a literal mountain, and its many component parts, this book utilizes a literal mountain and its various aspects as a metaphor to discuss the life experiences of humans and the many challenges humans face. As diverse is the makeup of the thousands of mountains in the world, so is the multiplicity of the life experiences of billions of human beings. All humans are destined to experience the ups and downs as part of this journey we call life. As one goes through life, the issue should not always be what one goes through, but rather the qualities of the person having emerged as a result.

This point of "outcome" is the driving message in this book. The information and exercises in this book are intended to function as a tool to inform, educate, inspire, and motivate individuals and groups toward understanding oneself and others through a literal or figurative mountain climbing experience. The active process and purpose of this book is to engage the reader in a journey from reader to dreamer to achiever.

Life is Like Climbing a Mountain was the selected title of this book since literal mountains are universal and almost everyone can identify with a mountain, a literal mountain, that is. In fact, much of the world's population lives in the mountains. As an aside, the topic of mountains elicits one of those circular thinking trivia questions, like what came first, the chicken or the egg? The question that emerges from this topic is: do people surround mountains, or do mountains surround people? Hmmm! The answer to this question is not a prerequisite for reading on, so, read on.

This book, "Life is like climbing a mountain" teaches the do's and don'ts for climbing an actual mountain. There are many different kinds of mountains in the world, and each mountain requires a different preparation in order to ensure a pleasant and rewarding climbing experience. The author hopes that the reader will gain insight from the reading and eventually garner the inspiration and qualifications necessary to climb a real mountain. The author further wishes that the reader will recognize the similarities in the requirements necessary to climb an actual mountain as compared to the skills humans require for surviving the challenging virtual mountain experiences of daily living.

This book will conclude with a question of what are the reader's personal (or organizational) dreams, goals, aspirations, and challenges. The question to the reader is: What is your mountain? The author refers to challenges as figurative or virtual mountains to be climbed. Also included at the end of the book is a working exercise or framework to help the reader/explorer identify and define his or her virtual mountains with a specific plan to map out and then climb a particular mountain or mountains. The purpose of the exercise is to encourage positive personal or organizational change. Some of the features to be changed, and perhaps by default, will be changed, include attitude, methodology or approach, environment, and sometimes entire plans. For instance, one might desire to climb an actual mountain; however, one's medical doctor says that that idea is in fact impossible given the patient's present physical health.

Chapter Two

The Act of Climbing a Mountain

There are peaks and there are valleys. High above are clouds and deep below are oceans. Life's journey is the challenge of climbing the mountains. There are thousands and thousands of mountains in the cosmos; each has its own unique character. No two mountains are alike. Like mountains, there are thousands and thousands of challenges in our lives of which to climb. The numerical idea of thousands is merely presented here in order to allow some degree of imaginative perspective, for the true number of mountains presented within the life of just one individual may be in the millions. Baby's first step represents a mountain climbed and achieved, surpassed only by the success of the next step. Some say that one's successful birth unto the earth is the first mountain climbed and achieved; the second is the drawing of one's first breath; the first suckling, the first hour of life outside the womb might be considered the third mountain climbed. Though every newborn experiences these mountains, not every newborn reaches these seemingly natural peaks of success. Victims of miscarriage or unsuccessful births, stillbirth, respirators, feeding tubes, birth defects, and those that do not survive the night all offer painful testimony. Among those who successfully reach these peaks, some reach it at various moments while others achieve successful assents with varying degrees of difficulty. These mountains that are seemingly the same present different challenges to different newborns. Stop here for a moment and try to think of the many mountains you've climbed before you even reached the age of five.

Perhaps mountains were created to be climbed and explored, to measure the explorer's faith, will, effort, energy, and skills. For some people, mountains appear to be larger than they actually are. Conversely, for others, mountains are viewed at eye level and are measured by the amount of time it takes to be climbed.

All who desire to climb a mountain do not necessarily aspire to reach its peak. It's understandable if one desires to not reach the top. That's acceptable because climbing to the top does not affect the composition of the mountain. Mountain climbers climb mountains for all different reasons. For instance, some will climb because they know in their heart and spirit that they can, in fact, reach the top; for them, the journey is not a challenge. Others will attempt the climb because they know that it is a challenge, and that they require the kind of challenge that measures their will and strength. Others will heed the calling because they are encouraged by others; their focus and efforts exist mainly for the benefit of others so the self-gratification value may not be as genuine. Then there are those mountain climbers who heed a more spiritual calling in search of one's self, a higher awareness, that profound experience – that epiphany. Perhaps when you really think about it, we've been climbing mountains since before we were born. Perhaps each of us is a mountain climber from birth.

Chapter Three

Understanding the Virtual Mountain Climb

This book presents the term "climbing a mountain" in the context of a challenge. According to Funk and Wagnall's New International Dictionary of the English Language, ©1995, the meaning of the word 'challenge', amongst others, includes: "To invite or defy". These terms are the terms on which this book is postured. In other words, one is invited to climb a mountain, literally or figuratively, as in maneuvering through life with a determination to defy the obstacles and threats that come with the experiences. According to the same dictionary, the term 'defy', means "To resist successfully". For this book, this definition will be expressed in terms of resisting the thought of "failure" and declaring "victory" according to one's personal or organizational aspirations and achievements.

While climbing a real mountain, as well as living life, one should expect sudden changes of events to occur. Life challenges or virtual mountains are simply natural parts of life. Some obstacles will come with warning while other challenges will just seem to appear. Unexpected changes will often require an entirely new set of workable plans in order to advance. A well traveled path on a mountain might become suddenly interrupted as a result of a collapsed huge tree that has impeded the mountain climber's trail. The mountain climber might instantly require an alternative trail in order to continue the climb. A couple to be married might feel that a huge tree has crashed their wedding plans when the limousine that was scheduled for a 2pm pick up will not be arriving.

In these two examples, the facts are clear that the huge tree has fallen and interrupted the mountain climb, and the limousine will not be taking the couple to the wedding ceremony. The challenge or virtual mountain in these two examples produces the question: what can or will be done by the actors in order to move forward? Should the mountain climber, who is so determined to reach the top of the mountain, turn around and go home, or should the climber seek an alternative trail? Of course, the mountain climber should assess the feasibility of going over, under, or around the tree. The climber might consider a plan to backtrack down the mountain until an alternative trail to the top can be successfully traveled.

For the couple to be married, should they cancel the wedding just because the limousine did not show up? Of course not, they should, like the mountain climber, assess the feasibility of the other alternatives towards declaring victory. For instance, they could use their personal vehicle, or they could phone a friend or even call for a taxi. In this case, the goal is greater than the means.

Each of the challenges, bouts, thrills, or experiences will need to be approached with the mastery of skills or appropriate tools that will make the mountain climbing experience more pleasant and achievable. Now, some of these skills will be natural, or previously attained (based on prior exposure), while other skills must be acquired, learned, and then mastered. Some of the tools can be self-managed while some tools will require the assistance, guidance, and/or cooperation of others.

Chapter Four

Climbing the Literal and Virtual Mountain at the Same Time

This book presents a typical instructional mountain climb using a literal mountain and its component parts as a metaphor to navigate one through a virtual mountain climb of typical life experiences. Actual instruction will be provided for someone who has never climbed a literal mountain. A systematic approach to climbing a literal mountain will be presented first, followed by an application for climbing a virtual mountain, which is, navigating through the challenges of life.

The intent of the exercise is to relate the experiences of an adventurous mountain climber to that of an individual or organization that faces challenges in the pursuit of achieving goals or, let's say, trying to climb a virtual mountain.

Many of the terms and jargon used in the world of mountain climbing are referenced in the glossary section of this book and are confirmed by an experienced mountain climber whose story also appears in this book. Further references can be made from the Glossary of Climbing Terms provided by Wikipedia, the free encyclopedia. These climbing terms will be applied appropriately in the scenarios that pertain to examples of real life situations.

For instance, the principal exercise depicted in this book features a person who faces a job search and possible career change. Susan has just celebrated her 35th birthday. She is now unemployed since the Insurance Company she served for ten years was recently purchased by a similar company in India. Susan really enjoyed her job as an assistant manager of operations, and was quite shocked to learn about the purchase and sale transaction of her company. Susan is now faced with the challenges to either find another job that will enable her to utilize her work experiences or consider a change in her profession – a virtual mountain.

Here we also meet Robert, a 20-year old young man who has always dreamed of climbing a mountain. He never quite figured out exactly why or what it took to safely climb a mountain, all he knew was that he wanted to climb a mountain – a literal mountain.

Okay, sounds like Robert and Susan will be adventuring a mountain climb. The difference is that Robert will be on a literal climb while Susan will be adventuring a virtual climb.

For Robert:

1. Determine the why, the what, the how, the when and the where concerning the mountain to be climbed.

Determine and explain why he wants to climb a mountain. What kind of mountain? Is he doing this for himself or for someone else? How important is climbing a mountain to him or someone else? When does he want to climb a mountain? Where is the mountain? What will happen if he doesn't get to climb a mountain? Who will climb with him? Will he climb alone?

To Susan:

1. Determine the why, the what, the how, the when and the where concerning the mountain to be climbed, in other words, the new job or the career change.

Susan has already determined why she needs to seek another job. She is still young, so she has to continue to work. Susan has to determine what kind of job she will seek. Will it be a job in the same field of insurance? Will she settle for a position and less pay than what she was used to? Will her decision be made for herself or for someone else? How soon will Susan be willing to work? Where or how far is she willing to go for a new job or new career? What will happen to Susan, short term or long term if she doesn't get a job or change careers? Who will help Susan pursue a new job? Will Susan pursue a new job by herself?

For Robert:

> 2. How many different physical mountains are there to choose from?

> Research and consider all the different kinds of mountains that are feasible for him to climb, based on locations, sizes, personal physical stamina, and safety.

For Susan:

> 2. How many different virtual mountains (jobs) are there to choose from?

> Research and consider all the different kinds of careers that she is considered qualified for based on experience, skills, and locations.

For Robert:

> 3. Define mission, and place value on achieving mission.

> Determine how committed he is towards reaching his goal or mission to climb a literal mountain. What is his plan of action? How knowledgeable is he for what is needed or required to climb the mountain that he has previously chosen? What will climbing a mountain ultimately mean to him?

For Susan:

> 3. Define the mission to find a job, and place value on achieving that mission.

Determine how committed she is to acquiring a new job. What is her plan of action? How knowledgeable is she for what is needed or required to get a job that is of interest to her? What will getting a job in her qualified field or even in a new career mean to her?

For Robert:

4. Predetermine the physical, mental and spiritual fitness required for the task of climbing a mountain.

Predetermine his physical, mental, and spiritual well-being after he determines and considers all that is involved in climbing a mountain that he so badly wants to climb. He must determine if he will be up to the task.

For Susan:

4. Predetermine the physical, mental and spiritual fitness required for the task of climbing a mountain, seeking a new job or a new career.

She must make sure that she will be physically and mentally able to carry out physical tasks associated with a new job, especially after she has come to understand the demands for the actual job search as well as the new job and new career.

For Robert:

5. Devise a back-up or contingency plan.

Devise a back up plan just in case he does not get to climb

the particular mountain that he desires to climb. Be flexible and willing to consider an alternative mountain.

For Susan:

5. Devise a back-up or contingency plan.

Devise a back-up plan. She should have a flexible and workable back up plan that will include other job descriptions and possibly other careers options, especially if her specific job interests and opportunities are not available.

For Robert:

6. Selecting your mountain? Assess and understand the environment.

Now that Robert has selected his mountain, he must investigate and learn the history of the mountain, understand the present conditions and consider the projected or future plans for this mountain. He needs to understand the environment of the specific mountain he intends to climb. Robert needs to be knowledgeable about new trails, and learn why former trails are no longer used. He should consider the industry trends in terms of mountain climbing. Robert should learn the latest models and product designs in climbing tools, gear, survival devices and equipment, and technology. Just as important to knowledge is all the component parts of the mountain that have to do with plant life, wild life, insects, rock formations and weather patterns. After Robert learns what to expect, he should learn how to properly use his five senses to recognize certain signs or patterns of situations that might otherwise be detrimental to him. For instance, he should be able to recognize poisonous plants, or dangerous animals or insects.

Robert should be able to distinguish the footprint of a bear or a moose. In fact, before climbing his chosen mountain, he should know if bears or moose roam this mountain. He should be able to determine if an animal's footprint is fresh or old. Robert should be able to distinguish the near and distant sounds of animals versus humans. Prior to his climb, he should become aware of weather patterns and the sudden temperature changes. Robert needs to devise an exit strategy from his mountain climb, especially if he begins his climb and decides that this particular mountain is not for him, or perhaps he might be better off climbing a different mountain.

For Susan:

6. Select your mountain (job or new career). Assess and understand the job market environment.

Now that Susan has determined the specific job or career change that she wants at a particular company, she must research and learn the history of the company. She should analyze the present environment. Susan should ask herself, Why is this company seeking someone to fill the position for which I am applying? How old is this company? Is this position new, or will I be replacing someone? If I am replacing someone, why is that person no longer there? Did that person get promoted, demoted, fired or did that person quit? Will that person be returning? If so, and if I take this job, will I have to leave if that person returns? If I am replacing someone, how long was that person there?

Susan should investigate the working environment. She should look at the work ethics, morale, loyalty, customer relationship management, company related commendations versus complaints. These company-related features are important to Susan because these qualities might influence her decision to proceed with her job application. Additionally, these features might eventually impact Susan's employment tenure, if she is hired or accepts the job. She should listen to what other employees are saying about the job and upper management.

In addition to the current conditions, Susan should study the company and the industry trends. Is the company growing? Is the company financially solvent? What are the company's missions and goals? Is the company on track towards meeting its missions and goals? If Susan intends to remain in the insurance field, she should investigate the latest licensure, certification, or continuing education or competencies, as required by the company, the industry, local, state of national government. Susan should learn the most up-to-date changes in the insurance laws and regulations if she plans to continue her career in insurance. She should brush up on the latest computer software and technology.

Like Robert, Susan will need to know how to use her five senses within her new environment. In other words, she will need to be able to see the signs of change. Apparently, Susan was a bit oblivious to warning signs at her other job. As an assistant manager, she should have noticed the frequent company meetings, the gradual downsizing of some of the offices, and the hiring freeze. As in the case of Robert's literal mountain climb, Susan should have a listening ear for the different sounds in the environment. For instance, Susan should listen for the workers that are happy and for the workers that complain. Susan must do as Robert did; she should devise an exit strategy in case she eventually determines that this particular job or company is not the mountain that she wishes to climb.

For Robert:

7. Being flexible sometimes requires changing positions or gear (clothing). In other words, sometimes one has to be able to wear more than one hat, or assume more than one role.

Robert's literal mountain climb will require patience on his part and from others who might journey with him. Robert will have to wear gear such as special shoes or boots, a heavy backpack filled with food, climbing tools, first aid supplies, water bottle and more. Robert might find that, after about the first half hour of carrying this extra weight, he begins to have second thoughts about his dream of climbing a mountain. He has to be flexible about his mission. Sometimes he will have to pick up the pace and move quickly, and keep a certain momentum. If Robert has decided to adventure with others, he might find that he might be asked to take a lead role in the mountain climbing venture. Other times he will be required to follow the veteran climbers.

For Susan:

7. Being flexible sometimes requires changing positions (job descriptions); sometimes one has to be able to wear more than one hat, or assume more than one role.

Susan's search for a job will require some flexibility and patience on her part. She will have to be flexible as she might find that some jobs that are of interest to her will require some skills that she does not have. She might need to acquire additional certification, or might need to accept a lower starting wage. Other opportunities might require her to start working part-time for a given period with a chance, but no guaranty, that she will be hired for full-time employment.

Susan will have to have patience in her job search. She might find what she feels is the perfect job, but when she contacts the company; she might learn that the position has been filled. Or, she might be interviewed, only to eventually have two follow-up interviews before she receives a "Thank you for your interest in the position, however..." letter or no response at all.

Susan's job search has been successful; let's applaud Susan for her new job as an Insurance Manager. She will need to be flexible and patient again. She might be asked to perform tasks not listed in her formal job description. For example, Susan might be asked to sit in for the receptionist who will be absent for three days. She might be asked to help stuff envelopes that have to be mailed out immediately, or she might be required to expeditiously learn the company's manual and policies that have a great deal of facts and figures.

For Robert:

8. Do not be afraid to talk; tell others about your plans, but be selective.

Robert has always dreamed of climbing a mountain. He has often mentioned his desire to others, but with no real conviction or plans. If Robert is really serious about climbing a mountain, he should talk about it to people who have the same interests. In fact, he should have substantive discussions with people who have mountain climbing experiences. A word of caution, however, should be given to Robert; he must be selective about who he talks to about his interests.

If he talks to someone who has negative views or thoughts, Robert's dreams could get shattered. In fact, Robert could get discouraged and might lose interest altogether in climbing a mountain. If Robert talks to the right person who could be supportive, he could learn a lot about what to expect from a mountain climbing adventure. Talking to others who are truly supportive of you is a part of the phase of building one's confidence and knowing your personal support system. Talking to others who are more knowledgeable about your interest is part of the phase of learning and understanding the environment.

For Susan:

8. Do not be afraid to talk; tell others about your plans, but be selective.

Susan, in her job search or career change, can use the same advice that Robert received concerning his mountain climbing adventure -- which he should not be afraid to talk and tell others about his plans. Likewise, Susan should be cautioned to be selective in the people or person she speaks to regarding her job search. A job search or a pursuit for a career change can be a sensitive topic, especially to someone who does not mean Susan well. If Susan speaks to someone that is negative, Susan's chances for a new job or career could be damaged. Conversely, if Susan speaks to the right person concerning her interest, her job search could be short lived. If Susan feels comfortable sharing her interest with others, then she could explain her situation and her level of flexibility regarding the terms and conditions for getting a new job or starting a new career. In fact, talking to others is a part of the understanding the environment phase. In Susan's case, insight concerning the people, the history, and future plans about a particular company could work to Susan's benefit. In fact, a supportive person may utilize her/his internal network of contacts to either or both locate a suitable position that Susan may not otherwise be aware of as well as provide a referral resource to get Susan an interview. On the other hand, the lack of information about certain people, an available position, or a company's environment could lengthen her search and harm her experience.

If Susan is to be congratulated for getting her new job, then she should also be encouraged to not be afraid to talk to others at the new job about her employment plans. Again, she should be selective about who she talks to. Positive information in the wrong hands could be detrimental. Conversely, positive information in the right hands could be a benefit, in this case, to Susan.

For Robert:

9. When climbing the mountain, one must understand the value and importance of occasional silence. For instance, if there are strange noises or sounds in the mountains, one should stand still, listen, look and observe, and then behave accordingly. Sometimes the best response is to stand still, move slowly, run forward or away. Consider the response options as they relate to the goal to climb the mountain. Before a decision is made, gather as much information as possible, but do not lose sight of the goal to climb the mountain. If possible, try to have patience during the process. Sometimes the sound might be a harmless passing wind. A hasty move could prove detrimental to the climber.

Before Robert begins to climb the mountain he will concede

that the ground that he will be treading on is new ground and new territory. As Robert begins his mountain climbing adventure, he will first look in the forward direction, and then upward, and then downward, to the ground, to understand his directional posture. He might eventually realize that he has perhaps never before looked down to the ground as much as he might feel the need to do so for this mountain climb. Robert also realizes that the new ground that he will be traveling will not be level, solid, necessarily smooth or free of matter that could distract him or could even cause him to stumble and fall. In fact some parts of the path might be pitfalls.

Robert's climb (if solo) will require that he, at times, practice being silent so that he can listen and hear his surroundings at different junctures. For instance, he might have to control the sound of his breathing, footsteps, or if he should be tempted to sing aloud, so that he could hear the flow of water, or the presence of birds, animals or other humans.

If Robert hears unusual and threatening sounds, he should try to quickly assess the situation and behave accordingly. He should decide if he should stand still, move slowly, run forward or away. If Robert decides to stay and confront whatever made the unusual and threatening sounds, the question becomes, has he prepared and equipped himself with the appropriate tools for protection? If he decides to move slowly, has he predetermined which safe direction he will go? Or, if he determines that he should run forward or away, what will that mean for his personal goal? If his plan to climb a mountain was to please or appeal to someone else, what will his decision to run forward or away from the unusual and threatening sound mean to others? Will the decision to abort the mountain climb be replaced by a determination to regroup at another time, and eventually complete the climb?

Robert should consider his lifelong dream to climb a mountain in his decision-making process, and what that will mean to Robert.

For Susan:

9. When climbing the mountain, literal or virtual, one must understand the value and importance of occasional silence. For instance, if there are strange noises or sounds in the mountain, one should stand still, listen, look and observe, and then behave accordingly. Sometimes the best response is to stand still, move slowly, or run forward or away. Consider the response options as they relate to the goal to climb the mountain. Before a decision is made, gather as much information as possible, but do not lose sight of the goal to climb the mountain. If possible, try to have patience during the process. Sometimes the sound might be a harmless passing wind. A hasty move could prove detrimental to the climber.

Susan's virtual mountain or goal is to get another job as a manager in the insurance field. She is determined to learn from her past experience of working for a company that was eventually sold to a company based in another country. Susan's ten-year management position at her former company seemingly offered her a sense of security, which for her ultimately proved to be not the case. She wants to be more sensitive to the job search and retention experience. So the advice to Susan for her pre- and post-job search is the following: While she is looking for a job, consider the skill of being silent. Silence, in this context, is the act of being focused and attentive to what is going on in the insurance industry and specifically with some companies that might be recruiting workers. Listen carefully to what is being said.

Assess what is being said, so that one can understand what is being said through the "buzz" or noise within the insurance industry. Once Susan gathers as much information as possible, and has an idea of what is being said, she can decide if she should stand still, move slowly, and run to or away from the job prospect. While her decision is being contemplated, she should focus on her mountain or goal to re-enter the insurance field.

Susan will get the advice that Robert received; if possible, try to have patience during the process. Sometimes the sound might be harmless or inconsequential, and a hasty decision could prove detrimental. In other words, she should make sure that the information or sound that she is hearing pertains to her, and that the "noise" is significant enough to warrant a shift of interest away from either the job that is being offered or the industry at large.

Susan should recognize as Robert did that the new ground that she will be traveling will not necessarily be smooth. There might be objects (people or bureaucracies) that could be on her "mountain's path" and impede Susan's job application and ultimately here employment opportunities. So, Susan will be encouraged to not only look forward and upward, but she should be cognizant of the ground that she treads. She should be aware of the pitfalls and traps that could cause her to be distracted and stumble.

Silence for Susan while job searching might mean that she has to refrain from displaying her upset or anger about her former job loss. If Susan decides to stay and confront the sound makers or the pitfalls, the question is then: does Susan have appropriate skills and tools for her defense and protection? If Susan decides to move slowly, has she devised a safe alternative for a job or career? In light of the noise or sounds that were heard by Susan, if she decides to run forward or away from the job prospect, what will that mean for her goal to acquire a new job or career? What will that mean to her or to others? Will a decision from Susan to abort an insurance job prospect be replaced by a determination to pursue or continue the search at a later date as part of fulfilling the goal to climb a virtual mountain, that is, for Susan, a job or career change?

Susan should consider the recommendation for occasional silence even after she gets a   job. She can exercise some of the same behaviors while she navigates through her new   job. From time to time she will hear noises, or information in the workplace that will appear threatening or offensive. Susan will need to make a decision to react based on   the information she gathers from her experiences. A hasty move could cost Susan her job. Susan's decision-making process should take into account her goal to climb a virtual mountain, by getting a management level job in the insurance field. Susan should assess what that will mean to Susan.

For Robert:

10. Remember that there are bears, wolves, and snakes in the mountain. There are also trees and rocks on the verge of falling.

Robert's excitement about climbing a mountain might blind him to the inherent dangers that exist in the mountains, dangers that could affect the quality of a good mountain climbing experience. At the moment that Robert determines that, yes, he will climb a mountain; he should consider the prospect of the whole experience. A thorough investigation of life and times of mountain climbing will reveal that every mountain has its share of wild life and other forms of movement. Robert should remember that on the mountain he decides to climb, there might be bears, wolves, moose and snakes, to name a few. There might also be trees and rocks on the verge of falling. So, he has to be particularly careful to avoid exposure to danger as he ascends and descends the mountain.

For Susan:

10. Remember that there are bears, wolves, and snakes in the mountain. There are also trees and rocks on the verge of falling.

During Susan's job search (virtual mountain climb), she will encounter obstacles that will affect her job search experience. For example, she might have to deal with making repeated telephone calls to inquire about a job opening, and might have to leave several messages. She might never get a return call. There might be other applicants or employees vying for the position she wants. Susan might have people around her, family members included, that might envy her and would rather see her fail.

Let's assume that Susan is successful at her job search, and gets a job in a desired field; she should still be aware of the negative people within the company. The falling rocks and trees are the company's policy and rule changes that are designed to upset and disturb Susan's spirit or morale. Susan should be concerned for her job security. She has to be especially careful to avoid exposure to the dangers of the other falling rocks and trees, such as the ones like the sudden changes in personnel, or the plans to expand, downsize, outsource, sell, or file for bankruptcy. Susan should be cognizant of these potential dangers as she ascends and descends the virtual mountain - job search, job find or career change.

For Robert:

11. Will you climb your mountain(s) alone?

A decision to climb a mountain alone is a very serious matter, particularly for Robert since he has never climbed a mountain before. He has to consider the extra challenges he might face, especially if he is not adequately equipped with the knowledge and the mountain climbing tools that are appropriately designed to ensure a successful climbing experience. If Robert decides to climb the mountain alone, that decision might be the right decision for him. In fact, if he does successfully climb the mountain alone, the results might be a demonstration of Robert's will and determination to succeed at achieving a life goal or dream. Conversely, if he decides to climb the mountain alone, then he will have assumed the inherent risks, that could prove detrimental or fatal. He should consider the knowledge value from the more experienced, or let's say, veteran mountain climbers.

For Susan:

11. Will you climb your mountain(s) alone?

A decision to climb a mountain alone is a little different for Susan than was the decision for Robert. For instance, Robert's ultimate decision could determine his fate, whereas, for Susan, her decision is not a matter of life or death. Susan's job search could be assisted by others, or she could decide to conduct the job search alone, since she has been in the workforce for many years. Susan could expand her job search opportunities if she is assisted by job search or employment agencies. In this case, she would not be climbing the mountain alone. If Susan is called to a job interview, normal protocol would warrant that she sit in the actual interview alone. So, in this instance, climbing a mountain alone could be a good thing.

For Robert:

12. Sometimes climbing a mountain alone could be difficult.

If Robert ventures to climb the mountain alone, he might encounter the natural or the wildlife dangers that are inherent in a mountain climb experience. He should consider the "what ifs" or the unknowns that might emerge during the climb. What if he is attacked by a bear? What if Robert is approached by a snake? What if he falls and is severely injured? These are issues that should be considered; otherwise, Robert's mountain climb experience could be difficult.

For Susan:

12. Sometimes climbing a mountain alone could be difficult.

Susan's virtual mountain climbing experience, seeking a new job or career change, could be hampered if she is oblivious to the value of additional help in her job search or career change. Like Robert, if Susan attempts her virtual mountain climb– alone, she might encounter the natural dangers inherent in a job search or career change experience. For instance, she might not know the latest interview techniques or 'buzz words', cultural norms, new industry innovations and processes or acceptable protocol within a certain job field or industry. Without good coaching, advice, or warning for what may be expected, for Susan may face additional challenges of discrimination or other forms of bias. These experiences could negatively impact her virtual mountain climbing experience. Susan could possibly minimize the potential difficulty that might be associated with a "lone" journey, if she receives favorable recommendations or credibility worthy references.

For Robert:

13. Make sure you are equipped to travel the mountain with the appropriate tools and supplies, because without the proper navigational tools, you might get lost in the mountains. Do not ignore visible danger signs; you might suffer and perish.

Robert's desire and determination to climb a mountain must be justified and clarified according to the specific kind of mountain that he will plan to climb. His research will inform that there are different kinds of mountains. For instance, there are tree mountains, rock mountains, ice mountains, and snow mountains. Each mountain requires different tools.

Robert will also discover that he will need different kinds of supplies based on the kind of mountain that he will climb. Robert should make sure that he understands how to properly operate navigational tools, or at least understand mountaineering techniques that help to provide a sense of directions, otherwise, he might get lost in the mountain. Robert should be attentive to the visible signs of safety and the signs of danger; otherwise, he could suffer and perish. For instance, he should learn what to do if fog begins to block his up-close and distant view. He should know what to do if rain begins to fall and the temperature begins to drop

For Susan:

13. Make sure you are equipped to travel the mountain with the appropriate tools and supplies, because without the proper navigational tools, you might get lost in the mountains. Do not ignore visible danger signs; you might suffer and perish.

When Susan sets out to job search, or to climb her virtual mountain, she will want to make sure that she is equipped with the appropriate tools, such as an updated resume, credible personal references, and appropriate attire. The navigational tools that she will need include the location and directions to the interview site, information about her interviewing format (she'll need enough resumes and reference sheets to hand to each interviewer), a clear understanding for the kind of job for which she is applying, and professional job readiness skills. Susan will benefit from knowing as much as possible about the company and the interviewer, so that she will not be lost in the interview if she is questioned specifically about the company. After a successful hire, Susan will need to navigate through the job or the new company. She could benefit from prior knowledge about the mission and goals of the company. Prior knowledge about a company and its operations will help Susan anticipate some of her experiences on the job. She should be able to recognize visible danger signs, such as staff reductions or a loss of customers. Without the knowledge and appropriate actions, Susan could suffer and perish on the job.

For Robert:

14. As you climb the mountain, do not forget your upward path. You might have to travel the same path to return to ground zero or to regroup.

When Robert sets out to climb his chosen mountain, he must not lose focus of the path he's traveling. He has to be flexible to enough to deviate, if necessary, around what would normally be obstructions or obstacles, such as trees or large rocks or even streams or brooks, even the unknown, unanticipated ones. Robert has to keep his eyes stationed towards the height of the mountain, and remember the characteristics of his upward journey's path. Robert's mountain climb might require that he retreats to the starting point of the mountain for the sake of regrouping in order to reassess a different methodology for climbing. If he has to return to the staring point of the mountain, he should recognize the required return as a learning experience, so that his subsequent climb or climbs will be fortified with his prior mountain climbing attempt.

For Susan:

14. As you climb the mountain, do not forget your upward path, you might have to travel the same path to return to ground zero to regroup.

This particular point for Susan is similar to the saying "Don't burn your bridge because you might need to travel it again." As she travels her virtual mountain in her job search or career change, Susan should always be reminded of her journey. She should acknowledge all of her experiences, the lessons to be learned, and the people she meets along the way. She just might have to one day recall her experiences, apply the lessons learned, call or reference the people she meets or even call upon them for recommendation or reference.

For Robert:

> 15. As you begin to approach the higher levels of the mountain, towards the top, the sunlight will become more intense. Sometimes the glory of the sun becomes too much to bear, and you might have to pull back and humble yourself.

As Robert climbs his literal mountain of choice, and assuming he picked a day when the sun is shining, he will notice that the higher up the mountain he ascends, the brighter the sky will be. Robert will also realize that the higher he climbs; the rays of the sun will seem to be more dramatically intense. At some point, he will attempt to resist the sunbeam in his eyes or the heat on his head. He might retreat and withdraw from the heat exposure. To avoid the direct heat, he might resort to a more shaded path that will allow him an uninterrupted journey towards the top. Depending on his tolerance of the conditions, and if they threaten his health or safety, Robert might surrender and abort his climb and descend the mountain.

Conversely, Robert's literal mountain climb might present him with rain showers or falling snow. The rain conditions could, in fact, darken the sky, and therefore put a "damper" on Robert's mountain climbing experience.

Similar to the conditions regarding the heat from the sun, the rain or the snow might drive Robert back down the mountain. The weather conditions involving the sun, rain, or the snow might challenge Robert to make a decision whether or not he will continue his climb in the midst of Mother Nature. He might decide to rest and wait awhile to see if conditions change to allow him to better manage the heat, falling rain or snow with less difficulty. His decision might lead him to resign from his mountain climbing efforts. Robert might concede at that point that he was not fully equipped or prepared to climb that particular mountain, on that particular day. He might later regret that he did not investigate the weather forecast that would have informed him about the sun, rain, or snow.

For Susan:

15. As you begin to approach the higher levels of the virtual mountain towards the top, the sunlight will become more intense. Sometimes the glory of the sun becomes too much to bear, and you might have to pull back and humble yourself.

Susan's recent job loss has forced her to climb a virtual mountain, vis-à-vis to find a like or similar job, or a new career. To advance her job search experience, let's assume that Susan has located, interviewed and started her new job. So as she begins to approach the higher levels of management, the prestige and the pressures of high standards and great expectations for performance and production will come with the territory of being a manager.

As in Robert's case of climbing the literal mountain, at some point Susan might experience an extraordinary amount of "heat" or pressure from upper management. In fact, the pressure from the top might be intense enough to force Susan to withdraw, and if conditions get so bad, she might resign or quit. Another way to view the point being made here is this: as Susan approaches the higher level of management, she might be overwhelmed with her title, authority or salary and benefits. If Susan is not careful, she could be perceived as a dictator, arrogant, and egotistical. The status of having rank and file might sometimes conflict with someone's ability to lead effectively. If that quality for Susan is the case, then she might want to pull back, humble herself, and remember why she is there at that job.

For Robert:

16. Sometimes it's advisable to seek shelter from the sun's rays.

As Robert prepares and actually begins to climb his mountain of choice, he has finally realized part of his life's dream -- to climb a mountain. The fulfillment of his dream, however, is to climb to the top of a preferred mountain. His momentum and upward journey towards the mountain top has been challenged by the sun's rays that temporarily impede his vision. He knows that the direct rays from the sun will slow him down, even if he wears sunglasses. Nevertheless, Robert is determined to complete his climb.

Robert should understand that seeking shelter from the rays of the sun is wise; especially if he accepts the idea that "sheltering from the rays of the sun" is part of the climbing experience. Sheltering, in this case, might mean that Robert will pause and sit in the shade until he feels he can continue his journey. What should be most important to Robert is his focus and determination to be successful at his climb, even if the climb is delayed by the sheltering.

In the case of Robert's literal mountain climb and the discussion of sun rays as a potential impediment to his climb experience, the facts could be easily changed to the act of rain or snow, but the reaction to accept the rain or the snow, as part of that experience, should be the same.

For Susan:

16. Sometimes it's wise to seek shelter from the sun's rays

Susan's virtual mountain climb as a manager on her job might require her to seek "shelter" from her senior managers or directors, if she gets orders and directives from them that might seem unbearable, unreasonable, ambiguous, even conflicting with corporate policy or the law. As she nears the virtual mountain "top, she might feel like the virtual rays of the sun (management's orders and directives) are impeding her vision, and will therefore impede her momentum for growth in the company.

If Susan somehow feels overwhelmed by the orders and directives from upper management, she might want to pause and assess what is happening and then determine how and when she should respond. In this case, the act of pausing and assessing the situation before moving forward becomes the "sheltering from the virtual rays of the sun or the rain or the snow". Susan might realize that taking the necessary reflection or "sheltering from the sun's rays" was important towards her overall goal to successfully move to a position of upper senior management. Susan should understand that taking the necessary pause, or seeking shelter, was a product of her being focused and determined to succeed at her virtual mountain climb experience.

For Robert:

17. How many mountains are in your life?

Robert has always aspired to climb a literal mountain, but what kind? For Robert, the specific kind of mountain really doesn't matter. As he begins to research the subject of mountains, he will discover that there are thousands and thousands of different kinds of mountains worldwide. For instance, there are tree-based mountains, snow-covered mountains, Rocky Mountains, dirt-based mountains, and ice mountains. Robert might consider eventually climbing a mountain of each kind. He might even desire to climb the known world's largest mountains. Robert is guaranteed to have a different mountain climbing experience for each mountain that he climbs. He will find a need to possess special tools for a safe climb. Also, he will need to be masterfully skilled to handle the expected and the unexpected challenges throughout his literal mountain climbing experience.

In real time, Robert can climb only one literal mountain at a time. While climbing the literal mountain of choice, Robert would be advised to focus on his journey to ensure his safety, and better his chances for a successful climb. Since the discussion here concerns Robert's literal mountain climb, a converse discussion concerning virtual mountain climbing will be held regarding Susan's virtual mountain climb; she will demonstrate the challenges of climbing more than one virtual mountain at a time.

For Susan:

17. How many mountains are in your life?

The number of mountains, virtual in Susan's case as she ventures to secure a new job or a new career, can appear to be countless. For example, her mountain or challenge can be manifested in her decision-making process as she contemplates the kind of job to which she aspires. A mountain for Susan could be the dilemma that she might face when she has to select between three job offers. If Susan considers a career change, a virtual mountain might be the need to satisfy all the application and educational requirements that are necessary for acceptance and passage. Unlike Robert's limited one mountain climb at a time, Susan can succeed at the challenges of climbing several virtual mountains all at once.

Like Robert, Susan is guaranteed to have a different mountain climbing experience for each virtual mountain that she climbs. She will find a need to possess special tools for a safe virtual climb. Also, she will need to be masterfully skilled to handle the expected and the unexpected challenges throughout her experiences getting the new job or new career.

While climbing her virtual mountain, Susan would be advised to focus on her journey, her job search, to ensure her safety and better her chances for.

For Robert:

18. How big are your mountains?

When Robert decided to pursue his aspiration to climb a mountain, he had to think about what kind of mountain he wanted to climb. Of course, he would learn about the different mountains from other people or from his own research. Robert would also need to consider when he would like to climb, where he would like to climb, and the size mountain he would like to climb. For some avid mountain climbers, the value of the climb is somehow determined by the size (how big or how high) the mountain is. The size of the mountain could determine many of the parameters for the journey. For instance, a high and steep mountain could require special shoes or boots, or extra food, because the journey will be longer than if for a smaller mountain. Before Robert begins his literal mountain climb, he should know how big is the mountain he wishes to climb.

For Susan:

18. How big are your mountains?

Before Susan sets out to climb her virtual mountain, Susan will need to consider in advance how big a job search she wants to entertain. She should try to predetermine if the mountain she chooses to climb is worth climbing. She will need to identify all the tools she will need based upon the size of the mountain she is determined to climb. In contrast to Robert's experience, Susan's virtual mountain climb will invariably include a consideration of the social, educational, and other human resources as tools, as well as the skills and personality characteristics that will support her successful mountain climbing experience.

For instance, if Susan is determined to change careers, she would want to understand the size of her virtual mountain, as it relates to her career change. Susan needs to be honest with herself and ascertain if the virtual mountain she aspires to climb is, in fact, the size that she would be determined to climb. The overall size of Susan's virtual mountain will dictate the qualifications and skills she would need to ensure her success. For instance, if she was interested in a new career that called for a Master's Degree, and she was really set on that particular career, well, she would have to work to achieve that level of education. Obviously, without that required credential, Susan would not be able to climb that virtual mountain. Throughout Susan's virtual mountain climb, she will have to constantly evaluate her positioning, in other words, the progress she has made, where she is, and the distance she must go towards completing her virtual climb.

For Robert:

19. What is your mountain?

By now, Robert has had a chance to research, understand and consider the many different kinds of literal mountains. He has had an opportunity to speak to veteran mountain climbers to learn of their experiences. Robert has studied the various histories, and environments of different mountains. Additionally, he has learned what specific tools and skills he needs to climb the various mountains. Robert has assessed his mountain climb aspiration and his capabilities and has made a final determination what is his mountain. Robert has taken ownership in climbing his mountain.

For Susan:

19. What is your mountain?

Susan now understands the concept of a virtual mountain climb. A literal mountain climb venture has been used as a metaphor to demonstrate the intricacies of climbing a real, literal mountain. She understands that her recent job loss has posed certain challenges, and those challenges have become the mountains that she must climb and conquer. Unlike Robert, who aspires to climb a literal mountain of choice, Susan is somewhat motivated to climb certain figurative or virtual mountains, or master required challenges in order to achieve desired successes. For instance, Susan has determined that she wants to pursue others job opportunities in the same field of insurance, as she was once a manager. She has recognized that practically all the nuances involved with her reestablishing herself will become somewhat a small mountain or process that is necessary towards reaching her defined mission.

Susan has had an opportunity to speak with other professionals in the insurance industry about their experiences. She has investigated the histories, current industry and environmental conditions, and the prospective trends for the insurance industry in her region. Additionally, Susan has familiarized herself with the new set of professional skills and credentials she will need that will make her virtual mountain climb a success. She has adopted the spirit to be flexible while she ventures the process of seeking a job; Susan has determined that if the job market or opportunities are not exactly conducive to her aspirations, then she would be willing to pursue other related job prospects. In fact, Susan would be willing to investigate other careers.

Susan's willingness to understand, adopt and adapt to the constantly changing environment has enabled her to define what her mountains are. Susan has taken ownership in climbing her mountain.

The purpose of the above exercise is to encourage positive personal or organizational change. Some examples of the encouraged changes include attitude, methodology or approach, environment and sometimes entire plans. For instance, one might desire to climb an actual mountain; however one's medical doctor says that that idea is in fact impossible-given the patient's present physical health.

The intent behind a mountain climb venture is to experience a transformation. For some people the experience produces an effect that invariably changes one's self confidence, and at minimum, the experience places a new lens and view on one's horizon. The new attitude demonstrates a spirit that says "**I CAN, I WILL,** and eventually, **I DID!**"

Chapter Five

Glossary of Climbing Terms

From Wikipedia, the free encyclopedia
This page describes terms and jargon related to climbing and mountaineering.

A
American death triangle
> A type of climbing anchor known for its weakness due to the physics of its construction.

Ablation zone
> The area of a glacier where yearly melting meets or exceeds the annual snow fall.

Abseil
> The process by which a climber may descend a fixed rope. Also known as *Rappel*.

Adze
>A thin blade mounted perpendicular to the handle on an ice axe that can be used for chopping footholds.

Alpine start
>To make an efficient start on a long climb by packing all your gear the previous evening and starting early in the morning, usually well before sunrise.

Altitude sickness
>A medical condition that is often observed at high altitudes. Also known as *Acute Mountain Sickness*, or AMS.

Anchor
>An arrangement of one or (usually) more pieces of gear set up to support the weight of a belay or toprope

Approach
>The path or route to the start of a technical climb. Although this is generally a walk or, at most, a scramble it is occasionally as hazardous as the climb itself.

Arête
>An outside corner of rock. Also a method of indoor climbing, in which one is able to use such a corner as a hold. See also dihedral.

Ascend
>To complete a route or problem.

Ascender
>A device for ascending on a rope.

ATC
>A proprietary type of belay device. (A subtle play on fact that ATC also stands for *Air traffic controller*.)

B

"B"-grade

> A grading system for bouldering problems, invented by John Gill. Now largely superseded by the "V" grading system.

Bachar ladder

> A piece of training equipment used to improve campusing and core strength.

Back-clipping

> A hazardous mistake that can be made while lead climbing. The belay rope is clipped into a quickdraw in the wrong direction causing an increase in friction on the rope and an increase in the likelihood of the rope becoming unclipped during a fall.

Bail

> To retreat from a climb.

Barn-dooring

> Swinging out from the wall like a door on a hinge.

Belay

> To protect a climber from falling using a rope, friction, and an anchor.

Belay device

> A mechanical device used to create friction when belaying by putting bends in the rope. Many types of belay device exist, including ATC, grigri, Reverso, Sticht plate, eight and tuber. Some belay devices may also be used as descenders. A Munter hitch can sometimes be used instead of a belay device.

Belay slave

> Someone that volunteers for, or is tricked into, repeated

belaying duties without partaking in any of the actual climbing.

Bergschrund (or **schrund**)

A crevasse that forms on the upper portion of a glacier where the moving section pulls away from the headwall. Also called a 'shrund.

Beta

Advice and/or instructions on how to successfully complete a particular climbing route.

Beta flash

Ascent of a climb on the first attempt with some knowledge beta of that climb, with no falls or hangdogging. Also see on-sight.

Biner

See Carabiner.

Bivy (or bivvy)

A camp, or the act of camping, from "bivouac." On a big wall, camp can be made on a natural ledge or an artificial one, generally a cotlike device called a portaledge that hangs from anchors on the wall.

Bivy-bag

A lightweight garment or sack offering full-body protection from wind and rain.

Bollard

A large knob of rock or ice used as a belay anchor.

Bolt

A point of protection permanently installed in a hole drilled into the rock, to which a metal hanger is attached, having a hole for a biner or ring.

Bolt chopping

The deliberate and destructive removal of one or more bolts.

Bomb-proof anchor

A totally secure anchor. Also known as a *bomber*. Anchors are often misclassified as such.

Bouldering

The practice of climbing on large boulders. Typically this is close to the ground, so protection takes the form of crash pads and spotting instead of belay ropes.

Bridging

see Steming

Bump

To quickly move up a hand or a foot a small distance from one useful hold to another.

Bucket

A large handhold.

Buildering

The art of climbing on buildings, which is often illegal.

Buttress

A prominent feature that juts out from a rock or mountain.

C

Cairn

A distinctive pile of stones placed to designate a summit or mark a trail above treeline.

Cams
> A spring-loaded device used as protection.

Campus
> The act of climbing without using any feet.

Campus board
> Training equipment used to build finger strength and strong arm lock-offs.

Carabiner
> Metal rings with spring-loaded gates, used as connectors. Also known as *crab* or *biner*.

Chalk
> A compound used to improve grip by absorbing sweat. It is actually *gymnastics chalk*, usually magnesium carbonate. Its use is controversial in some areas.

Chalk bag
> A hand-sized holder for a climber's chalk that is usually carried on a chalkbelt for easy access during a climb.

Chicken Head
> see bollard, horn.

Chimney
> A rock cleft with vertical sides mostly parallel, large enough to fit the climber's body into. To climb such a structure, the climber often uses his head, back and feet to apply opposite pressure on the vertical walls.
> The process of using such a technique.

Chipping
> Improving a hold by permanently altering the rock. Widely

used in the 80's and early 90's, but now considered unethical and unacceptable.

Chock _
>A mechanical device, or a wedge, used as <u>anchors</u> in cracks.
>A naturally occurring stone wedged in a crack.

Choss _
>Loose or "rotten" rock.

Classification _
>See <u>Grade</u>.

Clawing _
>Use of front points of <u>crampons, ice axe</u> pick and <u>ice hammer</u> pick to climb a slope.

Clean _
>To remove equipment from a route.
>A route that is free of loose vegetation and rocks.
>To complete a climb without falling or resting on the rope. Also see <u>redpoint</u>.
>In aid climbing, abbreviated "C", a route that does not require the use of a hammer or any invasive addition of protection (such as pitons or copperheads) into the rock (see <u>protection</u>).

Cleaning tool
>A device for removing jammed equipment, especially <u>nuts</u>, from a route. Also known as a *nut key*.

Climbing area
>A region that is plentiful with <u>climbing routes</u>.

Climbing command
>A short phrase used for communication between a climber and a <u>belayer</u>.

Climbing gym
> Specialized indoor climbing centers. See gym climbing.

Climbing shoe
> Footwear designed specifically for climbing. Usually well fitting, with a rubber sole.

Climbing technique
> Particular techniques, or moves, commonly applied in climbing.

Climbing wall
> Artificial rock, typically in a climbing gym.

Clipping in
> The process of attaching to belay lines or anchors for protection.

Col
> A small pass or "saddle" between two peaks. Excellent for navigation as when standing on one it's always down in two, opposite, directions and up in the two directions in between those.

Cordelette
> A long loop of accessory cord used to tie into multiple anchor points.

Corner
> An inside corner of rock, the opposite to an arête (UK). See Dihedral.

Cornice
> An overhanging edge of snow on a ridge.

Couloir
> A steep gully or gorge frequently filled with snow or ice.

Crack climbing _
> To ascend on a rock face by wedging body parts into cracks,
> i.e. not face climbing. See jamming and chimney.

Crag
> A small area with climbing routes, often just a small cliff
> face or a few boulders.

Crampons
> Metal framework with spikes attached to boots to increase
> safety on snow and ice.

Cramponing _
> Using crampons to ascend or descend on ice, preferably with
> maximum number of points of the crampon into the ice for
> weight distribution.
> Accidentally piercing something with a crampon spike.

Crank _
> To pull on a hold as hard as possible.

Crash pad _
> A thick mat used to soften landings or to cover hazardous
> objects in the event of a fall. *See*: Bouldering mat

Crater _
> Hitting the ground at the end of a fall instead of being caught
> by the rope.

Crimp _
> A small but positive hold, with very little surface area. See
> also Nub.
> The process of holding onto a crimp.

Crux
> The most difficult portion of a climb.

Cut-loose
> Where a climber's feet swing away from the rock on overhanging terrain, leaving the climber hanging only by their hands. Also known as "Cutting feet."

Cwm
> (Welsh) Hanging valley, cirque: a steep-walled semicircular basin in a mountain; may contain a lake, Cwm as does a corrie.

D

Daisy chain
> A special purpose type of sling with multiple sewn, or tied, loops. It is significantly weaker than a normal sling.

Dead hang
> To hang limp, such that weight is held by ligament tension rather than muscles.

Deadman anchor
> An object buried into snow to serve as an anchor for an attached rope. One common type of such an anchor is the snow fluke.

Deadpoint
> A dynamic climbing technique in which the hold is grabbed at the apex of upward motion. This technique places minimal strain on both the hold and the arms.

Deck
> The ground.
> To hit the ground, usually the outcome of a fall.

Deep Water Soloing
> Free climbing an area that overhangs a deep enough body of water to allow for a safe fall.

Descender
> A device for controlled descent on a rope. Many belay devices may be used as descenders, including ATCs, eights, or even carabiners.

Dialled
> To have complete understanding of a particular climbing move or route.

Diamox
> A drug used to inhibit the onset of altitude sickness. Otherwise known as *Acetazolamide*.

Dièdre
> A dihedral.

Dihedral
> An inside corner of rock, with more than a 90-degree angle between the faces. See also corner and arête.

Direct aid
> A type of tension climbing consisting of using one or more belay ropes to haul the leader up to the next point of protection.

Downclimb
> To descend by climbing downward, typically after completing a climb.

Dry tooling
> Using tools for ice climbing like crampons and ice axes on rock.

Dulfersitz _

 A method of <u>rappelling</u>, without mechanical tools, where the uphill rope is straddled by the climber then looped around a hip, across the chest, over the opposite (weak) shoulder, and held with the downhill (strong) hand to adjust the shoulder friction and thus the descending speed.

Dynamic belay _

 Technique of stopping a long fall using smooth braking to reduce stress on the protection points and avoid unnecessary trauma from an abrupt stop.

Dynamic rope _

 A slightly elastic <u>rope</u> that softens falls to some extent. Also tend to be damaged less severely by heavy loads. Compare with <u>static rope</u>.

Dynamic motion _

 Any move in which body momentum is used to progress. As opposed to *static technique* where three-point suspension and slow, controlled movement is the rule.

Dyno _

 A dynamic move to grab a hold that would otherwise be out of reach. Generally both feet will leave the rock face and return again once the target hold is caught. Non-climbers would call it a jump or a leap.

E

Edge

 A thin ledge on the rock.

Edging

 Using the edge of the <u>climbing shoe</u> on a foothold.

Egyptian

A climbing technique used to reduce tension in arms while holding a side grip.

Eight-thousander

A mountain that tops 8,000 meters.

Eliminate

A term from bouldering describing a move or series of moves in which either certain holds are placed 'off bounds' or other artificial restrictions are imposed.

Epic

An ordinary climb rendered difficult by a dangerous combination of weather, injuries, darkness, or other adverse factors.

Exposure

Empty space below a climber, usually referring to a great distance above the deck through which the climber could fall.

F

Face climbing

To ascend a vertical rock face using finger holds, edges and smears, i.e. not crack climbing.

Fall

Undesirable downward motion. Hopefully stopped by a rope, otherwise see mountain rescue.
A "free-solo belay," the quickest way to reach the ground.

Figure Four

Advanced climbing technique where the climber hooks a leg over the opposite arm, and then pushes down with this leg to achieve a greater vertical reach. Requires strength and a solid handhold.

Finger board _

Training equipment used to build finger strength.

First ascent _

The first successful completion of a route.

Fist jam _

A type of jam using the hand. See climbing technique.

Fixed rope _

A rope which has a fixed attachment point. Commonly used for abseiling or aid climbing.

Flagging _

Climbing technique where a leg is held in a position to maintain balance, rather than to support weight. Often useful to prevent barn-dooring.

Flake _

A thin slab of rock detached from the main face.

Flapper _

An injury consisting of a piece of loose (flapping) skin. A climber will usually just repair these with sticky tape or super glue.

Flash _

To successfully and cleanly complete a climbing route on the first attempt after receiving beta either by discussing the route or by watching another climber.

Follow _

What the second does.

Fourteener _

> Mountain that tops 14,000 feet in the contiguous United States.

Free climbing _

> Climbing without unnatural aids, other than used for protection.

Free Solo _

> Climbing without aid or protection. This typically means climbing without a rope.

Friction _

> Climbing technique relying on the friction between the sloped rock and the sole of the shoe to support the climber's weight, as opposed using holds or edges, cracks, etc.

Friend _

> A name brand of a type of spring loaded camming device (SLCD), sometimes used to refer to any type of spring loaded camming device.

Flute

> A usually insecure fin or flake of rock or ice.

G

Gaston _

> A type of climbing grip. Best described as a handhold thats is only good from the side, but you must hold it with your elbows pointing out.

Gendarme _

> A pinnacle or isolated rock tower frequently encountered along a ridge.

Geneva rappel _

> A modified dulfersitz rappel using the hip and downhill arm for friction, rather than the chest and shoulder, offering less complexity, but less friction and less control.

Glacier travel _

> Walking or climbing on a glacier; a rope is usually used to arrest falls into crevasses, but protection is not used.

Glissade

> A usually voluntary act of sliding down a steep slope of snow.

Gorp

> Trail mix for periodic nibbling to keep high energy level between meals on long climbs or hikes. An acronym for 'Good Ol' Raisins & Peanuts'

Grade _

> Intended as an objective measure of the technical difficultly of a particular climb or bouldering problem. More often is highly subjective, however.
> A surveying term for referring to the slope of an incline. (Grade (geography))

Grigri

> A belay device designed to be easy to use and safer for beginners because it is self-locking under load. Invented and manufactured by Petzl. Many experienced climbers advocate the use of an atc type device for beginners

Gripped _

> Scared. Also over gripping the rock.

Grovel _

>   To climb with obviously poor style or technique.
>   A climbing route judged to be without redeeming virtue.

Gumby _

>   An inexperienced (or unsafe) climber.

Gym climbing _

>   Climbing indoors, on artificial climbing walls. This is typically for training but many people consider this a worthwhile activity in its own right.

H

HACE

>   High Altitude Cerebral Edema - a severe, and often fatal, form of altitude sickness.

Hand traverse _

>   Traversing without any definitive footholds, i.e. smearing or heelhooking.

Hangdog _

>   While lead climbing or on top rope, to hang on the rope or a piece of protection for a rest.

Hanging belay _

>   Belaying at a point such that the belayer is suspended.

HAPE

>   High Altitude Pulmonary Edema - a serious form of altitude sickness.

Harness

>   See climbing harness. A sewn nylon webbing device worn around the waist and thighs that is designed to allow a person to safely hang suspended in the air.

Haul bag
> A large and often unwieldy bag into which supplies and climbing equipment may be thrown.

Head point
> *See top rope.* The practice of top-roping a hard trad route before leading it cleanly.

Headwall
> The region of a cliff or rock face that steepens dramatically.

Helmet
> Also known as a *brain bucket* or *skid lid.* It can save your life, but only while worn.

Hexcentric
> A protective device. It is an eccentric hexagonal nut attached to a wire loop. The nut is inserted into a crack and it holds through counter-pressure. Often just termed *Hex.*

Hold
> A place to temporarily cling, grip, jam, press, or stand in the process of climbing.

Honed
> To be in peak mental and physical fitness for climbing.

Hook
> Equipment used in aid climbing.
> A climbing technique involving hooking a heel or toe against a hold in order to balance or to provide additional support.

Horn
> Large, pointed protrusion of rock that can be slung. Typically also makes a good hand hold. See bollard, chicken head.

I

Ice axe

A handy tool for safety and balance, having a pick/adze head and a spike at the opposite end of a shaft.

Ice hammer _

A lightweight ice axe with a hammer/pick head on a short handle and no spike.

Ice screw

A screw used to protect a climb over steep ice or for setting up a crevasse rescue system. The strongest and most reliable is the modern tubular ice screw which ranges in length from 18 to 23 cm.

Ice piton _

Long, wide, serrated piton once used for weak protection on ice.

Indoor climbing _

See gym climbing.

J

Jamming _

Wedging a body part into a crack.

Jib _

A particularly small foot hold, usually only large enough for the big toe, sometimes relying heavily on friction to support weight.

Jug hold

A large, easily held hold. Also known simply as a *jug*.

Jumar
>   1. A type of mechanical ascender.
>   2. To ascend a rope using a mechanical ascender.

K
Klemheist knot
> An alternative to the Prusik knot, useful when the climber is short of cord but has plenty of webbing.

Knots

> Climbers rely on many different knots for anchoring oneself to a mountain, joining two ropes together, slings for climbing up the rope, etc.

L
Lead climbing
> A form of climbing in which the climber places anchors and attaches the belay rope as they climb.

Leader Fall
> A fall while Lead climbing. A fall from above the climbers last piece of protection. The falling leader will fall at least twice the distance back to her last piece, plus slack and rope stretch.

Lieback
> Or *layback*. A climbing move that involves pulling on the hands while pushing on the feet.

Locking carabiner
> A carabiner with a locking gate, to prevent accidental release of the rope.

Low-Angle _

>A face climb that is less than vertical; the opposite of an overhang or roof.

M
Mantle

>A move used to surmount a ledge or feature in the rock in the absence of any useful holds directly above. It involves pushing down on a ledge or feature instead of pulling down. In ice climbing, a mantle is done by moving the hands from the shaft to the top of the ice tool and pushing down on the head of the tool.
>
>The external covering of a climbing rope. Climbing ropes use kernmantle construction consisting of a kern (or core) for strength and an external sheath called the mantle.

Match

>To use one hold for two limbs, or to swap limbs on a particular hold.

Moat _

>A crevasse that forms where the glacier pulls away from a rock formation.

Mountain rescue

>A friendly team of people that may come and rescue you after an injury or accident. May also search for overdue climbers, at no small peril and expense. Also *see* coroner and rescue doctrine of negligence law.

Move _

>Application of a specific climbing technique to progress on a climb.

Moving together

> Method of climbing – used on easy Alpine ground – in which two or more climbers climb at the same time with running belays between them and fixed belays not being used.

Multi-pitch climbing

> Climbing on routes that are too long for a single belay rope.

Munter hitch

> A simple hitch that is often used for belaying without a mechanical belay device. Otherwise known as an *Italian hitch* or a *Friction hitch*.

N

Névê

> Permanent granular ice formed by repeated freeze-thaw cycles.

No-hand rest

> An entirely leg-supported resting position during climbing that does not require hands on the rock.

Nub

> A little hold that only a few fingers can grip, or the tips of the toes.

Nunatak

> A mountain or rock that protrudes through an ice field.

Nut

> A metal wedge attached to a wire loop that is inserted into cracks for protection. See hexcentric.

Nut Key

> See Cleaning Tool

O

Objective danger

> Danger in a climbing situation which comes from hazards inherent in the location of the climb, not depending on the climber's skill level. Most often these involve falling rock or ice, or avalanches.

Off-width

> A crack that is too wide for effective hand or foot jams, but is not as large as a chimney.

On-sight

> A clean ascent, with no prior practice or beta.

Open book

> An inside angle in the rock. See also dihedral.

Overhang

> A section of rock or ice that is angled beyond vertical. See roof.

P

Peak-bagging

> To systematically attain designated summits under prescribed conditions.

Peel

> To fall.

Pendulum

> Swinging on taut rope to reach the next hold in a pendulum traverse.

Pickets

> Long, tubular rods driven into snow to provide a quick anchor.

Picknick stop
> A No-hand rest.

Pinkpoint
> To complete a lead climb without falling or resting on the rope (hangdogging), but with pre-placed protection and carabiners. Also see clean and redpoint.

Pinch Hold
> This is a hold where you must pinch it to hold on. They come in various sizes.

Pitch
> In the strictest climbing definition, a pitch is considered one rope length (50-60 meters). However, in guide books and route descriptions, a pitch is the portion of a climb between two belay points.

Piton
> A flat or angled metal blade of steel which incorporates a clipping hole for a carabiner or a ring in its body. A piton is typically used in "aid-climbing" and an appropriate size and shape is hammered into a thin crack in the rock and preferably removed by the last team member.

Piton catcher
> clip-on string fastened to piton when inserting or removing, so as to avoid loss.

Plunge step
> An aggressive step pattern for descending on hard or steep angle snow.

Pof
> An alternative to chalk made from pine resin. Popular

in Fontainebleau but discouraged (or actively forbidden) everywhere else since it deposits a thick, shiny resin layer on the rock and friction can only be achieved by using more pof.

Positive _

Of a hold or part of a hold, having a surface facing upwards, or away from the direction it is pulled, facilitating use.

Pressure Breathing _

Forcefully exhaling to facilitate O2/CO2 exchange at altitude. Also called the "Whittaker wheeze".

Problem _

Used in bouldering, the path that a climber takes in order to complete the climb. Same as route in roped climbing.

Protection

Process of setting equipment or anchors for safety.
Equipment or anchors used for arresting falls. Commonly known as *Pro*.

Prusik

A knot used for ascending a rope. It is named after Dr Karl Prusik, the Austrian mountaineer who developed this knot in 1931.
To use a Prusik knot for ascending a rope.

Pumped

To have such an accumulation of lactic acid in the flexor digitalis (forearm), that forming even a basic grip becomes impossible. Often easy activities such as holding a camera become difficult or impossible.

Q
Quickdraw

Used to attach a freely running rope to <u>anchors</u> or <u>chocks</u>. Sometimes called "quickies" or just "draws."

R
Rack

The set of equipment carried up a climb; also, the part of a harness (consisting of several plastic loops) where equipment is hung, ready to be used.

Rappel

The process by which a climber may descend on a fixed rope using a friction device. Also known as *Abseil* or *roping down*..

Rebolting

The replacement of bolts on an existing climb.

Redpoint

To complete a <u>lead climb</u> without falling or resting on the rope (<u>hangdogging</u>). Also see <u>clean</u> and <u>pinkpoint</u>.

Rest step

Energy-saving technique where unweighted (uphill) leg is rested between each forward step, sometimes by "locking" knee of rear leg.

Retro-bolting

The addition of bolts to an existing climb.

Roof

Horizontal overhang.

Rope

A basic item of <u>climbing equipment</u> that literally connects the climber to the belayer.

Rope jumping
> Jumping from objects using rock climbing equipment.

Route _
> The path of a particular climb, or a predefined set of moves.

Runner _
> Another term for *sling*.

Runout _
> An inordinate span between two points of protection.
> A long portion of a route with minimal protection.
> The portion of a route between the last point of protection and the top anchor, typically a fairly low-grade slab.

Rugosity _
> Hold sized area of rock that has rougher texture than its surroundings.

RURP _
> Acronym, stands for Realized Ultimate Reality Piton. Miniature, postage-stamp sized piton originally designed by Yvon Chouinard

S
Saddle _
> A high pass between two peaks, larger than a col.

Sandbag _
> A climb which receives a much lower grade than deserved. A traditionally protected climb can, if undergraded, be very dangerous, and the term sandbag is often said with a note of respectful dread.

Scrambling
>A type of climbing somewhere between hiking and graded rock climbing.

Screamer
>1. A long and loud <u>fall</u>.
>
>2. A nylon webbing structure consisting of one large loop sewn up in multiple places to make a shorter length. In the event of a fall the sewn sections part, absorbing some of the fall energy and decelerating the climber.

Scree
>Small, loose, broken rocks, often at the base of a cliff.

Second
>A climber who follows the <u>lead</u>, or first, climber.

Self-Arrest
>The act of planting the pick of your ice axe into the snow to arrest a fall in the event of a slip. Also a method of stopping in a controlled glissade.

Send
>Cleanly completing a route. ie on-sight, flash, redpoint. Sometimes even on tr.

Serac
>A large ice tower.

Sewing machine leg
>The involuntary vibration of one or both legs resulting from fatigue or panic. Also known as "Scissor leg", "Elvis Presley Syndrome", or "Disco knee".

Sharp end

The end of the <u>belay</u> rope that is attached to the <u>lead</u> climber.

Short fixing

The <u>lead</u> climber switches over to self belaying and continues to climb after reaching a belay and fixing the rope. Meanwhile the second climber jugs the fixed rope and cleans the pitch. When he reaches the belay, he ties in and starts to belay the leader in the traditional way again. When the leader reaches the next belay the process is repeated.

Side grip

A (usually vertical) hold that needs to be gripped with a sideways pull. Often just simply called a "side pull."

Simulclimbing

A technique where both climbers move simultaneously upward with the leader placing protection which the second removes as they advance. A device known as a Tibloc which allows the rope to only move in a single direction is sometimes used to prevent the second climber from accidentally pulling the lead climber off should the second slip.

Sirdar

Head <u>Sherpa</u> mountain guide.

Sit start

Starting a climb from a position in which the climber is sitting on the floor. This is common in climbing gyms in order to fit an extra move into the climb.

Slab

A relatively low-angle (significantly less than vertical) section of rock, usually with few large features. Requires slab climbing techniques.

Slab climbing _
> A particular type of rock climbing, and its associated techniques, involved in climbing rock that is less than vertical. The emphasis is on balance, footwork, and making use of very small features or rough spots on the rock for friction.

Slack _
> Portion of rope that is not taught, preferably minimized during belay.

SLCD _
> Abbreviation for spring-loaded camming device; a type of protection device. These are better known by the term cam.

Sling _
> Webbing sewn, or tied, into a loop.

Sloper _
> A sloping hold with very little positive surface. A sloper is comparable to palming a basketball.

Smearing
> To use friction on the sole of the climbing shoe, in the absence of any useful footholds.

Snarg _
> A type of tubular ice screw that is inserted by hammering.

Snow fluke _
> An angled aluminium plate attached to a metal cable. The fluke is buried into snow, typically used as a deadman anchor.

Solo climbing _
> Setting and cleaning ones own protection on an ascent; climbing by oneself.

Sport climbing

A style of climbing where form, technical (or gymnastic) ability and strength are more emphasized over exploration, self-reliance and the exhilaration of the inherent dangers involved in the sport. Sport climbing routes tend to be well protected with pre-placed bolt-anchors and lends itself well to competitive climbing.

Spotting

An alternative to belaying commonly used during bouldering. A friend of the climber stands beneath them and prevents awkward falls or falls onto hazards.

Sprag

A type of hand position where the fingers and thumb are opposed.

Static

Of a style of climbing or specific move, not dynamic.

Static rope

A non-elastic rope. Compare with dynamic rope.

Stem

1. The simultaneous use of two widely spaced footholds.

2. Climbing using two faces that are at an angle less than 180° to each other.

Sticht plate

A belay device consisting of a flat plate with a pair of slots. Named after the inventor Franz Sticht.

Stick clip

A device used in sport climbing to clip the first bolt. This is especially useful if the first bolt is high up, and out of the comfort zone of the climber. A stick clip can be bought or easily made by attaching a quickdraw to a stick with a rubber band.

Stopper
1. A wedge-shaped nut.

2. A knot used to prevent the rope running through a piece of equipment.

Summit
1. The high point of a mountain or peak.

2. To reach such a high point.

Swami Belt
A kind of proto- climbing harness consisting of a long length of tubular webbing wrapped several times around the climbers body and secured with a water knot. Largely eschewed today in favor of commercial harnesses.

Swinging-lieback
A dynamic form of the lieback described above, rotating off one foot while maintaining a grip with that hand, then grabbing a high handhold at the deadpoint of the swing. This move is frequently reversible, unlike more aerial dynos.

T
Talus
Large rock fragments forming an often unstable slope below scree.

Teabagging
When, after a whipper, or long fall, a climber falls past their belayer, who is generally lifted up off the ground.

Technical climbing
>Climbing involving a rope and some means of protection, as opposed to scrambling or glacier travel.

Tension
>A technique for maintaining balance using a taught rope through a point of protection.

Thrutching
>Bad technique or 'body climbing' specifically at Mount Arapiles

Top rope
>To belay from a fixed anchor point above the climb.

Top-out
>To complete a route by ascending over the top of the structure being climbed.

Traditional climbing
>A style of climbing that emphasizes the adventure and exploratory nature of climbing. While sport climbers generally will use pre-placed protection, many traditional (or "trad") climbers will place their own protection as they climb, generally with a rack.

Tramming
>A technique that is typically used while cleaning gear from a steep route. A quickdraw is clipped between the climber's harness and the rope that is threaded through the gear. As the climber is lowered by the belayer, they will descend along the line of the gear.

Traverse
>To climb in a horizontal direction.

A feature of a route that allows relatively easy progress in a horizontal direction.

A *Tyrolean traverse* is crossing a chasm using a rope anchored at both ends.

A *pendulum traverse* involves swinging from a protection point.

Tricam

A piece of rock climbing protection.

Tuber

A belay device.

Tufa

A limestone formation, like a stalactite attached to the wall. eg "Mega Tufa Wall", Mallorca

U
Undercling

A hold or flake that is upside down.

V
"V"-grade

A technical grading system for bouldering problems, invented by John Sherman.

Verglas

A thin coating of ice that forms over rocks when rainfall or melting snow freezes on rock. Hard to climb on as crampons have insufficient depth for reliable penetration.

W
Wand

A bamboo stick with a small flag on top used to mark paths over glaciers and snow fields.

Webbing

Hollow and flat nylon strip, mainly used to make runners and slings.

Webelette

A piece of webbing with eyes sewn into the ends which can be used in place of a cordelette.

Weighting

As in, "weighting the rope." Any time the rope takes the weight of the climber. This can happen during a minor fall, a whipper (long fall), or simply by resting while hanging on the belay rope (see also hangdogging.)

Whipper

A lead fall from above and to the side of the last clip, whipping oneself downwards and in an arc. Has come to be the term for any fall beyond the last placed or clipped piece of protection.

Wired

To have the moves required for completing a climb memorized. See dialled.

Wires

A slang term for nuts.

Woodie

A home made climbing wall. Often specifically a hybrid between a climbing wall and a fingerboard. Specifically called such because of the wooden panels (usually left unpainted) used to attach the climbing holds to.

X

Y

Yosemite Decimal System

A numerical system for rating the difficulty of walks, hikes, and climbs in the United States. The rock climbing (5.x) portion of the scale is the most common climb grading system used in the US. The scale runs from 5.0 to 5.15a (as of 2005)

Yabo

Another name for a Sit start, a 'Yabo start' was named after John 'Yabo' Yablonski[1].

Z

Z-clipping

Clipping into an anchor with the segment of rope from beneath the previous anchor, resulting in an unsafe configuration of the belay rope.

Zipper fall

A fall in which each piece of protection fails in turn.

Z-pulley

A particular configuration of rope, anchors, and pulleys typically used to extricate a climber after falling into a crevasse

Chapter Six

Take a Literal Mountain Climb with Robert

The following fictitious story is designed to take the reader through a literal journey on a mountain climb. Included is an application of selected terms and jargon related to climbing and mountaineering. These climbing and mountaineering terms can be found in the Wikipedia, the free encyclopedia. The reader should realize that Wikipedia is just one of many sources that can inform in this genre. Therefore, the Glossary of Climbing Terms used in this book is neither conclusive nor exclusive of all the relative terms applicable in a climbing or mountaineering experience. Within the Glossary of Climbing terms, several terms are interchangeable. Some terms can be used to express the same meaning. What is hoped to be achieved from this exercise is a thorough education and a working knowledge of what one might experience before, during, and after climbing an actual mountain. In some instances, terms can be related to other types of climbs such as trees, rocks, ice or snow. If the reader is not familiar with the terms as they are used in the story, the reader is encouraged to revisit terms and jargon as provided in the section of Glossary of Climbing Terms. Throughout this story, the first use of the selected climbing terms will be italicized. If the intended point in this story needs to be better illustrated then in some cases, part or all of the definitions will be provided.

Robert finally decided to prepare himself and follow his lifelong dream to eventually climb a mountain. He read books, viewed movies that involved mountain climbing, and talked to avid, professional mountain climbers. Robert even studied the history of many mountains in the area. He joined a local gym and kept an active membership so that he would feel *honed,* to be in peak mental and physical fitness, for climbing. Robert underwent a simulated mountain climb at the local gym. He practiced the *climbing wall*, artificial rock, typically in a climbing gym. Robert practiced for several hours learning *climbing techniques*, particular techniques, or moves, commonly applied in climbing. In fact, he selected the specific mountain that he wanted to be his first mountain to climb. He knew that this particular mountain would be a distinguished *climbing area*, a region that is plentiful with climbing routes. With excitement and confidence, Robert felt *dialled* about his imminent experience; he had a complete understanding of his particular climbing move or route.

On the second day of April, Robert finally made up his mind that he would climb a mountain the next day. So he geared up with an *alpine start* to make an efficient start on a long climb, by packing all his gear the previous evening and staring early in the morning, usually before sunrise. He knew that he would be climbing a mountain that would present some challenges, so he was sure to wear his *climbing shoes*, footwear designed specifically for climbing. Robert drove his car for at least forty-five minutes before he reached the mountain site. He parked his car in the campground parking lot. From the parking lot, and at a distance, Robert could see the *approach*, the path or route to the start of a technical climb. Frozen in place, staring at the approach, and then at the height of the mountain, and then back at the approach, Robert kept remembering the *beta*, advice and instruction he received from his next door neighbor Michael. Michael advised Robert on some aspects of mountain climbing, and how Robert could successfully climb a particular route. With the *beta* from Michael, Robert had the confidence he could manage *beta flash*, his ascent of a climb on the first attempt with some knowledge of that climb.

Robert did his homework before he left for the climb. He studied the weather forecast for the day, which indicted that rain and strong winds would be expected. So he was sure to bring a *bivy-bag*, a lightweight garment or sack offering full- body protection from wind and rain. As Robert ascended his mountain climb, he noticed several possible paths or route from which to choose. To the left side of the route he saw a *cairn*, a distinctive pile of stones placed to designate a summit or mark a trail above the tree line. Continuing on his trail, Robert had to climb a large boulder. He mastered that. He was ever so happy for his short lessons on *bouldering*, the practice of climbing on large boulders. He noticed while climbing the boulder, he needed to secure his balance; he reached out to what he thought was a solid rock. In reality that rock was a *choss*, a loose or "rotten" rock. Apparently, someone at some point in time must have notice the *choss*, because right next to it was a *chock*, a mechanical device, or a wedge, used as anchors in cracks. After about one hour of rather easy climbing, Robert encountered an *epic*, an ordinary climb rendered difficult by a dangerous combination of weather, injuries, darkness, or other adverse factors.

Heavy rain began to fall. Robert's clear vision was impeded a bit. He searched for a *hold*, a place to temporarily cling, grip, jam, press, or stand in the process of climbing. His determination kept him motivated towards an upward climb. Just as he stepped outward to advance to another rock, Robert realized he had encountered *exposure*, an empty space below a climber, usually referring to a great distance above the deck through which the climber could fall.

Up to that moment of the climb, Robert did not face any greater threat of a *fall*. Robert focused on what he was there to do. He eliminated his fears and was able to continue his climb. He accomplished his *first ascent*, the first successful completion of a route. Up to this point in the climb Robert felt quite professional, and his experience was a *flash*: he successfully and cleanly completed his climbing route on the first attempt after receiving beta either by discussing the route or by watching another climber. Robert has felt that his skills for mountain climbing were demonstrated at a level that one could not call him *gripped*, scared, or *gumby*, an inexperienced (or unsafe) climber, or that his climb was *grovel*, to climb with obviously poor style or technique.

About two hours into the mountain climb, Robert attempted to step onto a boulder and his foot slipped. To keep from falling, Robert resorted to *jamming*, wedging his body part into a crack. This was just a temporary measure until he was able to regain composure for proper footing. He was soon on his way, and the mountain climb continued. This first climb for Robert will surely be one to remember. He eventually approached a portion of the trail that was blocked by a fallen tree, and the only way for Robert to advance on his journey was to consider a *move*, applying a specific climbing technique to progress a climb. Robert sensed that his climb was becoming more risky. He knew that he would have to resort to the use of *knots*; climbers rely on many different knots for anchoring oneself to a mountain, joining two ropes together, and slings for climbing up the rope. Robert was willing to take the risk of the *objective danger*, danger in a climbing situation which comes from hazards inherent in the location of the climb, not depending on his skills.

Most often these involve falling rocks, ice, or avalanches. Although he recognized that *solo climbing*, was his choice, Robert was nevertheless reassured that if he was met with a major challenge or grave danger, he could rely on a *mountain rescue*. They may also search for overdue climbers, at no small peril and expense.

After Robert secured the rope for an upward climb, he thought he had *on-sight*, a clean ascent, with no prior practice or beta. While climbing upward on the rope, the rope began to swing like the motion of a *pendulum*. Robert found it necessary to use a *nub*, a little hold that only a few fingers can grip, or the tips of the toes. With the rope in his hand, he had to use *tension*, a technique for maintaining balance using a taught rope through a point of protection. The surprise of this part of the climb taught Robert that no matter how well a *route* is planned; there will always be something that will be unexpected, such as blocked trails or paths. Eventually, Robert was successful in this challenging part of his climb. However, he did notice *scree*, small, loose, broken rocks. He was relieved to know that he did not have to deal with a *talus*, large rock fragments forming an often unstable slope below *scree*. To his immediate right, Robert saw a *buttress*, a prominent feature that juts out from a rock or mountain. Since this climb was his first climb, Robert could not claim this climb to be *wired*, to have the moves required for completing a climb memorized. When Robert prevailed over the climb related challenges, he knew that he would be on his way to the mountain's *summit*.

He was determined to accomplish his mountain climb, so he would never think about a *bail*, to retreat from a climb. At this particular point, Robert felt that he had experienced the *crux*, the most difficult portion of a climb. He began to feel a bit hungry, so he reached for his *gorp*, trail mix for periodic nibbling to keep high energy level between meals on long climbs or hikes. After having successfully climbed to the summit, Robert felt accomplished. He paused and reflected a moment then began his *downclimb*, his descent by climbing downward. Following the ascending route but in reverse, Robert eventually reached his parked vehicle, entered it and gradually drove off into the sunset.

Chapter Seven

Take a Virtual Mountain Climb with Susan

The following fictitious story is designed to take the reader through a journey on a virtual mountain climb. Opposite to Robert's actual mountain climb, Susan, while sipping on her morning coffee discovered that the insurance company where she worked for at least ten years had been acquired by another company based in India, and unless she was willing to relocate to India, she was lose her job. Moving to India was not an option for Susan. So Susan was forced to consider a virtual mountain climb. Her mountain climb would consist of pursuing another job in the same field or training for another new career or occupation. Like Robert's mountain climbing experience, this exercise applied selected terms and jargon related to climbing and mountaineering. These terms, however, were used in the context of Susan investigating and pursuing her life options with respect to her being gainfully employed again. In the case of Susan's virtual mountain climb, some key terms were selected to illustrate the parallel with Robert's literal mountain climb experience and Susan's virtual mountain climb experience. The climbing terms that were used in Robert's story were followed by the literal definition or meaning. The climbing terms that were utilized in Susan's experience, were followed by the appropriate meaning in order to bring understanding to the virtual mountain climb for Susan's new or restart on life. If the reader is not familiar with the terms as they are used in the story, the reader is encouraged to revisit the terms and jargon as provided in the section of Glossary of Climbing Terms. Throughout this story, the first use of the selected climbing terms will be first-letter capitalized and the entire word highlighted and italicized. If the intended point in this story needs to be better illustrated then in some cases, part or all of the definitions will be provided.

Unlike Robert's free-will decision to prepare for a literal mountain climb, Susan was somewhat forced to prepare to climb a virtual mountain. Her mountain has become her need to look into her future employment options. Susan investigated and assessed her different choices by understanding the history and trends of the industry where she worked prior to losing her job. Susan wanted to be *honed*, to be in peak mental and physical fitness for climbing. She needed to make sure that she was up to the search.

On the second day of April, as Robert did, Susan started her day with a virtual mountain climb to the local employment center. The night before, Susan meticulously prepared a general resume outlining her personal and professional qualities, accomplishments and attributes (her version of an Alpine start). She selected and prepared a professional portfolio with which to carry her resumes, notepad and writing instruments. She then selected and ironed a business suit that she would wear to the employment center. Susan gave considerable thought to her *approach* to her job search. While getting dressed, somewhat excited but anxious, Susan developed some anxiety and felt the urge to *bail*. She began feeling nervous about her virtual mountain climb plans, especially since she had neither applied for nor interviewed for a job in more than ten years. She contacted a friend for advice and instructions on how to successfully complete a job search. After careful instructions and a pep talk, Susan garnered confidence enough to go forward with the job search at the employment center.

Susan spent almost two hours looking at different jobs and career opportunities. In fact, there were two job recruiters there from a local law firm. The recruiter was seeking at least three individuals who might have interest in the legal field as a paralegal. These immediate positions would offer training and coaching for the appropriate certification. Susan began to think about her personal skills sets and then felt confident about the job search. With her *beta flash*, she decided to discuss this opportunity to train to be a paralegal. The recruiter offered Susan a practice interview opportunity, so that if she was really interested in the paralegal trainee position, she would be comfortable with the offering. For Susan this *bouldering* experience could be a benefit because it would help Susan overcome her nervousness, and not feel like she failed the interview. The practice interview was Susan's *climbing wall*; it would allow Susan to, if she had to fall, not become bruised. The employment agency was similar to a *climbing area*, a region that is plentiful with climbing routes, in that it offered many different job and career opportunities.

Throughout the actual interview, Susan kept on her virtual *climbing shoes*; she stood firm on her responses to the questions. The practice interview allowed Susan to learn *climbing techniques*, particular techniques, or moves, commonly applied in climbing. She was able to quickly respond to the questions with excitement about the potential career change. By the end of the interview, Susan had confidently *dialled*; she had a complete understanding of her climbing moves and route. The recruiter was so impressed with Susan's skills and interests that Susan was actually offered the position on the spot. Susan gladly accepted the paralegal trainee position with the understanding that she would have to train and acquire the appropriate certificates. She also knew that she would have to learn a new language as well – the language of 'legalese' or legal terms and terminology. She left the employment agency feeling like she had performed her *first ascent*, the first successful completion of a route. Thanks to Susan's friend for the pep talk for confidence and direction, along with the benefit of the practice interview, Susan experienced a *flash*.

Two weeks later, Susan began her virtual mountain climb of becoming a paralegal at the law firm. On her first day, Susan *gripped*; she was scared. She did not know what to expect or what to do. Perhaps she was considered *gumby* because she was inexperienced or because her behavior as a new employee was *grovel*, with obviously poor style or technique. Susan's first assignment was to accompany a small group of lawyers to court for an ongoing criminal trial. While in court Susan was to take notes of what was going on, and also to assist the lawyers as they needed certain documents. As the trial proceeded and the "heat was on", the Chief Counsel for the case began requesting certain documents, one after the other. The rapid requests became a bit overwhelming for Susan because she was not quite familiar with the different exhibits and documents. She called out for a virtual *mountain rescue*, and a few of the accompanying lawyers came to Susan's rescue to help her do her job. Susan had just learned a *move* to progress on her climb due to experiencing *objective danger*. Prior to becoming overwhelmed by the passing of the documents and exhibits, Susan experienced *on-sight*, a clean ascent, with no prior practice or *beta*. The lawyers from Susan's new job put before Susan a *route* to follow to be successful. To the lawyers, Susan was a *second*, a climber who follows the lead, or first, climber. This new job for Susan was never meant to be a *solo climbing*. For this virtual mountain climb, Susan determined that the *summit*, the high point, would be to get training and then to become duly certified as a paralegal.

Susan's training was *wired*; she had the moves required for completing a climb memorized. The training lawyers created learning routine that would help Susan to learn what she had to do. The *crux*, the most difficult portion of the climb, was the transition from being a manager to starting a new career that required new skills, new language and new tools. Susan's superiors encouraged Susan, often giving her *climbing command*, communicating with her and regularly reminding her that she could make it. The lawyers served as a *belay*, to protect Susan from falling. After six months of rigorous training and practice, Susan tested and passed her paralegal examination and was therefore awarded her paralegal certification.

Susan was well-liked at the law firm where she worked. She was able to apply many of the skills she knew from the insurance industry where she was an assistant manager. At her new job, Susan was offered a *buttress*, a prominent feature that juts out from a rock or mountain, a paid opportunity to pursue a career as a lawyer, if she wanted to aspire to climb that virtual mountain. This opportunity grew out of the opportunity to train to become a paralegal. Susan understands that if she plans to study to become a lawyer, she will have to consider *peak-bagging*, to systematically attain designated summits under prescribed conditions. In other words, before she can become a licensed attorney, she will have to meet other benchmarks, which become smaller summits or mountains. Before Susan can begin, she must approach a *problem*, the path that a climber takes in order to complete the climb. She must do this so that she will understand her options and a possible exit strategy, in the event that there is a change in plans.

Chapter Eight

The Significance of Mountains...
It's A Spiritual Phenomenon

Mountains, mountains, mountains. It seems no matter where you look, there are mountains; some high, some low. Mountains are all about us. It seems that they surround us, or if we think about it, do we surround mountains? Hmm, think about that for a while.

Let's consider the significant role that mountains have played in the whole caption of what we call life and the universe. From the stories that depict the beginning of time, as in creation, as in the existence of human beings, the mountain as an object has had a profound impact on and in our lives. Think for a moment how the mountain seems to represent a place for spiritual transformation or a place for a life-changing experience. A tremendous source of spiritual power seems to emanate from mountains. For instance, according to all bibles that recognize God as the Creator, the scriptures indicate that God spoke his words from the mountain. Many stories told throughout the Holy Bible involve characters that had profound life-changing experiences that occurred in the mountains. For example, Moses' life was changed when he received directives from God. Jesus Christ had remarkable life experiences in the mount.

We also see this theme in modern historical figures. Dr. Martin Luther King Jr. in his famous "I had a dream" speech said that he had been to the mountain top. The mountain of Mount Rushmore has meaning since some prominent former United States Presidents' statuesque faces adorn it. Literally, hundreds of songs crossing all lyrical genres include references to mountains. Rhythm and blues songs are performed to express that "ain't no mountain high enough, ain't no valley low enough..." In the American patriotic song, "My Country, Tis of Thee", the word mountain is referred to in the last stanza "...from every mountainside, let freedom ring". Even in the American national hymn, "America the Beautiful", reference is made to "purple mountains majesties..."

The Holy Bible (KJV) is replete with stories and scriptures that pertain to mountains. The selected stories and scriptures for this book represent instances where persons had profound life-changing experiences. These stories and scriptures demonstrate some of the life-changing experiences written about people from the deep and sometimes gloomy past, so that the reader/explorer can appreciate the trials and challenges that other people had. Hopefully others can be encouraged to believe through faith, works, and applied skills, that the challenges they face can be conquered. The stories of the literal mountain climbs should inspire the reader/explorer to investigate and assess the requirements to succeed in a personal virtual mountain climb.

To the reader/explorer: as you begin the process of trying to identify what your virtual mountain is and the level of faith and the non-physical tools you will need to add to the literal tools that are essential to achieving your goals or aspirations-at whatever level, consider the following scriptures of faith. As part of this exercise, everywhere you see the word 'mountain', replace it with the word that represents your personal goal or aspiration. For example, if your personal goal is to go to college, then going to college becomes your mountain. Now, completing college by a certain time frame becomes another mountain, attaining a certain grade point average becomes yet another mountain, and so on. Some or all of these mountains represent a different composition and set of required skills, and road maps. All of these mountains can be pursued simultaneously.

The following variations of terms, as variables, should be used to replace the word mountain found in the following scriptures when speaking about your specific virtual mountain climb.

A. My Dreams/Goals/Aspirations,
B. Challenge to my Dreams/Goals/Aspirations
C. Successes and Accomplishments to my Dreams/Goals/Aspirations

*Lord, by thy favour thou hast made my MOUNTAIN to stand strong: thou didst hide thy
face, and I was troubled. Psalm 30:7

*Every valley shall be exalted, and every MOUNTAIN and hill shall be made low: and the crooked shall be made straight, and the rough places plain. Isaiah 40:4

*Then was the iron, the clay, the brass, the silver, and the gold, broken to pieces together, and became like chaff of the summer threshing floors; and the wind carried them away, that no place was found for them: and the stone that smote the image became a great MOUNTAIN, and filled the whole earth. Daniel 2:35

*Who art thou, O great MOUNTAIN? before Zerubbabel thou shalt become a plain: and he shall bring forth the headstone thereof with shoutings, crying Grace, grace unto it. Zechariah 4:7

*And Jesus said unto them, because of your unbelief: for verily I say unto you, If ye have faith as a grain of a mustardseed, ye shall say unto this MOUNTAIN, Remove hence to yonder place: and it shall remove; and nothing shall be impossible unto you. Matthew 17:20

*Which removeth the MOUNTAINS, and they know not: which overturneth them in his anger. Job 9:5

*Surely the MOUNTAINS bring him forth food, where all the beasts of the field play. Job 40:20

*Therefore will we not fear, though the earth be removed, and though the MOUNTAINS be carried into the midst of the sea; Psalm 46:2

*Though the waters thereof roar and be troubled, though the MOUNTAINS shake with the swelling thereof. Selah. Psalm 46:3

*The MOUNTAINS shall bring peace to the people, and the little hills by righteouness. Psalm 72:3

*Before the MOUNTAINS were brought forth, or ever thou hadst form the earth and the world, from everlasting to everlasting thou art God. Psalm 90:2

*The MOUNTAINS skipped like rams, and the little hill like lambs. Psalm 114:4

*As the MOUNTAINS are round about Jerusalem, so the Lord is round about his people from henceforth even for ever. Psalm 125:2

*For the MOUNTAINS shall depart, and the hills be removed; but my kindness shall not depart from thee, neither shall the covenant of my peace be removed, saith the Lord that hath mercy on thee. Isaiah 54:10

*For ye shall go out with joy, and be led forth with peace: the

MOUNTAINS and the hill shall break forth before you into singing, and all the trees of the field shall clap their hands. Isaiah 55:12

*Oh that thou wouldest rend the heavens, that thou wouldest come down, that the MOUNTAINS might flow down at thy presence. Isaiah 64:1

*And though I have the gift of prophecy, and understand all mysteries, and all knowledge; and though I have all faith, so that I could remove MOUNTAINS, and have not charity, I am nothing. 1 Corinthians 13:2

*And every island fled away, and the MOUNTAINS were not found. Revelation 16:20

Chapter Nine

The Human Volcanic Mountain

What is a volcanic mountain, and how does volcanic mountains relate to human life?

To understand what a volcanic mountain is; we should understand what a volcano is. According to Funk and Wagnall's New International Dictionary of the English Language, (1995), a volcano is an opening in the earth's surface surrounded by an accumulation of ejected material, forming a hill or mountain, from which heated matter is or has been ejected: known in the former case as active and in the latter as dormant or extinct.

As humans, our life is sometimes a virtual active or dormant volcanic mountain that incubates positive or negative energy. The negative energy that humans produce poses a threat to the quality of our health, safety, and overall promise of life. The positive or negative energies may be manifested in individuals or government organizations.

Like literal volcanic mountains, at some point in time, all forces must be released. Some social issues might be perceived to impact international societies, while other issues might appear to concern local communities and individuals.

The daily stresses of wars, international terrorism, genocide, famine, poverty, oppression, global warming, and corrupted governments are only some of the problems that are projected on an international level. When these problems are compounded with other problems such as pollution, social injustice, religious persecutions and ruined economies, one might conclude that our existence as humans, at some point will be challenged. National or local issues that threaten the sense of community include: domestic violence, domestic murders, sickness and disease, unemployment, homelessness, crime, racism, sexism, discrimination, and rising energy costs, seem to stagnate the growth and development of local communities. To further add to the negative energy that seems to permeate our communities substance abuse and dependencies must be acknowledged. These and more issues contribute to the calamity that we as humans are heading towards.

With the pressures of life, we become stressed, depressed, violent, and suicidal. We suffer from lack of self-confidence, lack of self respect and love for others, and low self-esteem, envy, jealousy, hatred or contempt.

One way to view our life is as a virtual/spiritual volcanic mountain. We can perceive a volcanic mountain as a natural element that generates a mass of energy within. The fierce energy mounts within and becomes combustible, and will inevitably erupt. Like a literal volcanic mountain with pressures that can be released with a brutal force, we can sometimes experience similar pressures, sometimes violent, as a result of life's stresses.

A volcanic mountain that has the capacity to erupt at any point in time can manifest in a positive or negative manner. In fact, lava that spews from a bursting volcano can have a positive and a negative effect on the environment at the same time. For instance, to volcanologists, geologists, archeologists, and other related scientists, an active volcano serves as a positive event to the world of science that strives to understand the nature, behavior and after-effects of volcanoes. Conversely, to a thriving ecological system of wildlife, vegetation and human habitation, an active volcano has long-term negative effects on all the living matter that the ejected burning lava comes in contact with. Instant death is brought to all living organisms. In fact, not only is the immediate area exposed to the innate destructive lava that is released from the erupted mountain, but the hazardous volcanic smoke and airborne ashes that travel for miles and miles threaten and impact the air quality, ocean and sea life, area and distant animal and plant life for months, if not years, into the future. Again, human habitation and vegetation are negatively affected and threatened long-term as a result of a single eruption. A single volcanic eruption can precipitate several reactions that could result in more crippling damage to the environment.

Volcanologists, geologists, archeologists, and other interested scientists, might perceive an active volcano as a natural way to purge living organisms and purify the immediate land mass on which the erupted heated lava flows. These scientists might perceive the effects of an active volcano as a positive and acceptable way to restart habitation and vegetation, but not for years to come. This "purification" process might be perceived to have a similar effect on a land mass, similar to when farmers of sugar cane intentionally burn the sugar cane fields. After the sugar cane fields are set ablaze, the intense heat and smoke causes snakes and other field animals to flee the immediate area. To the spiritualists, this "purification" process also sterilizes the soil and allows for spiritual innocence to resurge. To the non-scientists, an active volcano, as a natural act or disaster is obviously not positive, but, in fact, negative, especially when a volcano threatens life of all forms. Nevertheless, after the hot lava cools and unique rock formations are defined, a new environment has been established.

As stated earlier, humans possess volcanic mountain-like characteristics. The intense pressures of life that are brought on by the "isms" of the world, and are cultivated within the human spirit often remain dormant, yet brewing, sometimes for years and years. Like the literal volcanic mountain, but as virtual spiritual mountains, humans maintain countless forms of negative energy (such as anger, hatred, envy, jealousy, fear, insecurity and contempt) until someone or something causes the virtual volcanic mountain to erupt. The explosion of a virtual volcanic mountain, as in the case of a physical volcanic mountain, will cause everything living and non-living in its path to be affected. When the human spiritual and virtual mountain erupts, perhaps a positive and a negative impact can be claimed. For instance, a positive impact might be embraced for the person who became purged of life's stresses.

As in the case of the volcanologists, geologists, archeologists, and other interested scientists who invited the literal volcanic mountain eruption, the virtual eruption might be perceived as welcoming and entertaining for some. Psychologists, psychiatrists, sociologists, social workers, pastors, or even parents, may consider the eruption of the human virtual spiritual volcanic mountain to calmly release the stresses of life that are continuously brewing. This hopeful position might be justified if the person who became purged of his/her life's stresses subscribes to the "purification" theory as was posited by the spiritualists, who held that a spiritual innocence could resurge following a sterilization of the land mass.

In this analogy involving humans, one might recognize a spiritual cleansing if this virtual spiritual volcanic mountain was able to release the negative energies sooner than later, as a way of minimizing future combustible forces that might cause greater catastrophic damages. To add to the positive view, if negative matter was released and caused no serious harm or threat to life, then the release of the volcanic material could without question be applauded.

However, if the virtual spiritual volcanic mountain erupted and the virtual lava spewed about and posed grave threats and actual long-term damage to people, especially innocent people, then the virtual volcanic event will have been recognized as negative.

Now, the virtual spiritual volcanic mountain, in the form of a human, can be viewed as a positive natural phenomenon. The power or energy that is generated and maintained within the human spirit could be recognized as positive pressure. This positive energy could become pressurized and later released as positive spiritual lava that has the innate ability to transfigure the life of the subject human virtual spiritual volcanic mountain, and positively impact other humans, as well as the immediate environment. The forms of positive energy that can be cultivated while dormant and within include: allegiance to God, love, caring, enthusiasm, faith, hope, compassion, charity, creativity, honesty, exercise, good nutrition, integrity, high self esteem, and self respect, humility and peace. If these qualities could be envisioned as the virtual volcanic smoke and ashes, once released, these qualities could become airborne and travel for miles and miles to ultimately affect other people and larger communities. Like the hot lava from the literal volcano that formed new rock horizons, when the lava cooled, new and improved social conditions would be established, and eventually the quality of life for all humans would be improved. The release of the internal positive pressure could be inspired or influenced by genuinely affording and engaging people to speak up and out for equality and justice for all. If these opportunities are presented to humans, as virtual volcanic mountains, and a positive eruption is encouraged, and the world is made to be a better place in which to live, then a virtual spiritual volcanic mountain eruption would not be so bad after all.

Chapter Ten

Chuck Peters' Story

The following story is shared, in the first person, by Mr. Chuck Peters who is an avid mountain climber. Chuck has climbed several hundreds of mountains during the past few decades. His detailed account of a particular physical mountain climb is offered for this book, so that the reader will recognize the application of the process for climbing a virtual mountain.

Towards the end of the twentieth century, I had visited Ireland for the first time. The entire week of my visit was great: great friends, great pubs, great views, great ale, great people, and, of course, great big stouts of more ale. The rolling hills, quaint villages, stunning views, expansive fields, and big mountains offered beautiful panoramas.

The Dreamer

During my return flight to the states, the thought of climbing one of Ireland's mountains happened upon me. Now, to most, this thought would fall into the 'passing' category; but to me, an avid mountain climber, this developed into a tantalizing thought, which quickly developed into a consuming thought. This, in turn, by the time we had landed and I disembarked the plane, became a mission.

Over the course of the year, I continued to pursue my joy of climbing while holding down a full-time job with a florist wholesaler. If you were to see or speak to anyone who both enjoys and actually physically climbs mountains, two very distinct facts will always be realized. The first is that the person has and continues to build a passion for climbing; the second is that s/he would be in great physiological and psychological condition. A climber is just as acutely aware that the opportunity to climb can happen sometimes at a moment's notice as one also knows the importance of being honed both physically and mentally in preparation for a climb – any climb. Your preparation to climb is as important to you as a solo-climber as it is to others as part of a team. I typically follow a strict weight, strengthening, and aerobic workout regimen as well as a variety of mental awareness, focusing, and overall mental health-strengthening routines. When you make a climb, you are, in fact, making two climbs: a physical climb and a mental climb. If you are not mentally prepared for the expected and unexpected rigors of a climb, your physical preparedness, even at peak conditioning, will be moot. I was ready. I wanted to climb a mountain in Ireland. It remained a burning desire in me throughout the year – even through other climbs.

My friends and I had just brought in 2001 in joyous celebration and we each were looking forward to a better year. I, personally, had a greater, internal reason to celebrate. Being single, having no steady girlfriend or children, and with a week off from work, I decided that it was time to finally fulfill my long-awaited passion, to execute and complete my 'mission' and climb one of the mountains I saw earlier in Ireland. The Friday evening before the start of my vacation was when I really began dreaming of mountains with a challenge. I immediately jumped online to Priceline.com in search of the cheapest airfare. I was able to secure a round trip ticket to Ireland at a very reasonable rate. Great! I leaned back my head, closed my eyes, and began mentally visualizing the mountain range I had seen during my earlier trip to Ireland. It was during this mental purview that I foretasted the particular mountain that would fulfill my mission and feed my passion. I would ascend and summit their high mountain.

After a wonderful and comfortable, yet long, flight, I finally arrived in beautiful Shannon. That night I spent a wild time with a couple of wild Irishmen in the local pub. I was hurting the following morning, but a splendid time was had by all. This was clearly not part of the mountain-climbing preparation experience but I was on vacation. I started out early in the morning and drove down to the Ring of Kerry where the high mountains of Ireland are. Before leaving for Ireland, I had pre-booked a 4-night bed and breakfast with a wonderful couple. I arrived late morning, settled into my room and began checking my gear. I would later head out in search of some local climbing and gear shops. As I stepped away from the bed and breakfast, I looked up at the mountain range and there I saw it – Mount Carrantuohill, their high mountain.

The Believer

Now I really didn't know much about Mount Carrantuohill so it was critical that I seek out and acquire some Beta. I knew, as mountains went, it wasn't a monster of a mountain at 3,416 feet. However, I knew nothing else including what to expect. I visited local climbing and gear shops, sought out topographical maps, and acquired climbing Beta from some experienced local climbers and non-climber locals who supplied historical and environmental information.

Now keep in mind the month was January, and Ireland rarely gets snow at ground level. Up in the mountains, is where vast amounts of snow will be found. This presents a bevy of other concerns --

ice, heavy winds, snow drifts, covered trails, and the many other often hidden, unforeseen dangers that impact a winter ascent of an unfamiliar climb. But I've climbed New Hampshire's White Mountains in winter before. White Mountains are some of the most aggressive mountains in the world in the winter time, but I was well-honed, ready, and dialled.

From the acquired Beta, I learned that there are not a lot of trails on Mount Carrantouhill to begin with and what trails there are remain unmarked. However, there are certain approaches that are common to most local and familiar, dialed climbers. The Beta providers had given me a tip for one side of the mountain that they suggested may offer the optimum approach for the climb. They even suggested that if I were to drive down this long dirt road, I'd end up at this farm where for fifty pence the farmer would let me park in his driveway. Having driven around the mountains a few times considering both the various approaches as well as all of my options, the suggested approach proved the approach of choice.

I returned to the bed and breakfast for the evening with a bottle of wine for my wonderful hosts. We would later pop the cork and enjoy it with some light conversation sprinkled with a bit of television. I was asked the reason for my visit here in Ireland, to which I responded, "Well, tomorrow I'm going to climb Mount Carrantouhill". The wife/hostess broke out in laughter. "No you're not, nobody climbs Carrantuohill in the winter time," she said. "Well, ah, I am. As a matter of fact, let's forget about breakfast in the morning because I'm going to have to wake up real early and get to the mountain", I stated. Once she realized that I was, in fact, serious, she tried for quite some time to talk me out of it. She was very concerned. So concerned was she that once she realized that she wasn't going to talk me out of it, she made me provide her my entire written itinerary: the side of the mountain I'd be climbing, the approach, the farm that I'll be parking at, what time I thought I would get on the mountain, what kind of summit, what time I'd thought I'd be back down – everything. She made it crystal clear that if I didn't call her within about two hours of the time I thought I would be down, she'd be calling out Search and Rescue for me. I retired to my room, geared up for an Alpine Start, and took in some sleep.

The next morning I awakened bright and early... well early anyway. You see, in Ireland during the winter months, especially January, the days are very, very short; in fact, it doesn't get light outside until about 8:30 or 9 in the morning while darkness falls around 4:30 or 5 in the afternoon. This presents a relatively short window of light with which to climb. So my plan was to start the approach in the dark and then once I hit the mountain, hopefully it would be dawn. Then I'd be able to summit and get back down, and not have to worry about climbing down the mountain in the dark. Believe me; descending in the dark at no time excites me.

All geared up, I headed downstairs and, much to my surprise, saw that the wife/host had gotten up extra early just to make me an extra large breakfast. She also made me a couple of cucumber and ham sandwiches to put in my backpack. I remember her coming over as I was just getting my gear together, kissing me on the forehead and gently saying, "You be safe, Yank, and when you come down you make sure you call me."

In retrospect, I suppose solo-climbing an unknown mountain in January might not have been the most prudent thing, but I was not to be denied. This was something I always dreamt of doing. There, inside me, it seemed a spiritual calling, greater than I was summoning me to the mountain. I always loved Ireland and the Celtic world, so I thought this would be just perfect. It had to be. I just couldn't turn back.

The Explorer

The Approach Begins

The rain seemed to get worse and the wind was coming up, so donning my full waterproof gore-tex gear, I put the rest of my gear on, my back pack, then headed off. Though fully prepared, before I could manage Beta Flash, I had to first manage the five-mile 'schlep' from the farm to the foot of the mountain. I say schlep because it was five miles of unrelenting mud, wet shale, and "poo". Believe me, when I get back, I will most certainly 'help' the locals in updating their "Poo Report" Beta. But, true to the Beta, there were no trail markers. I kept pulling out the topography map as I had plotted out sort of a course to go on by according to the Beta given me by the guys in the climbing shop. They had told me that during this climb there would be one point during the approach where I would have to cross what they called a brook. Good Beta is critical, I tell you. Well, needless to say because of all the rain and it being January, by the time I got to the brook, it had swollen so badly that the normal crossing point wasn't traversable. I had to walk about another half-mile downstream in order to find a place to cross.

I finally reached a crossing point, and realized that I was experiencing my first Epic moment of the climb. The water was flowing very well as the rain continued to pour heavily. I knew that I had to 'get wet' anyway, so I slowly waded knee-deep across the fast-moving current. Having made it safely across I found myself completely drenched. Now if this wasn't enough, I discovered that the back of one of my boots had totally blown out; the stitching had gone and I could see my sock through the back of the boot. I thought to myself, "This is great". However, being the good, well-prepared climber that I am, I opened up my back pack, grabbed some duct tape, and began wrapping my boot in duct tape as close to a water-tight seal as I was going to get out there. I gathered my gear then marched on.

Finding New Meaning

I continued hiking along, roughly four and a half miles in towards the approach, when I entered this ravine/valley called Hags Glen. The rain had pretty much subsided when I unexpectedly found myself surrounded by mountains on all three sides. The most awestruck, truly amazing sight to behold surrounded me. It was the most beautiful place I had ever been in my entire life. Small, speckled patches of blue magically appeared here and there all around me as the sun came through striking against the wet rock. It gave a glow, a surreal aura that I never experienced before in my life -- a quiet storm of color and calm. At that point, I realized that that climb was going to be the most beautiful climb I was ever going to have. As I think about the feelings I felt, I struggle to find the appropriate words to now express myself. It felt more like love than a climb; a sort of passionate welcome; a rapture of sorts. No longer did I feel like I was being tested by obstacles being thrown at me. I believe that that experience was an invitation and a gift; so, I sought to discover many such gifts along the way. Proceeding through Hags Glen, I could see the mountain approach that I would be taking. Looking up, I could see the ridge that I would have to hit first before I could see the peak, so I knew I was in the right place.

I happen to have a very high metabolism, so when I climb, I usually carry at least three quarts of fluids. For this climb, however, I decided to carry one quart of water, and two quarts of the local high-energy drink, a Gatorade knock-off they call Lucozade.

I slowed down and decided to drink some of the Lucozade. I have never drunk this energy drink before, but I was told that this would certainly give me a boost of energy when I needed it. I probably got about twenty-five percent of one quart bottle down when, almost immediately, I had an allergic reaction. My entire body rashed up and my face blew up like a balloon. A rash under my arms and between my legs had appeared to where any movement of my limbs yielded an awful, debilitating pain. Even my sight had been seriously compromised, as the rash had surrounded my eyes thus reducing them to mere slits. I thought, "This is crazy". I couldn't continue forward, yet there was just no quitting. This too, was a gift, though I didn't feel quite 'gifted' yet), so I just stopped there and waited it out.

Roughly forty-five minutes later, the rash and associated pain had subsided significantly. I could now open my eyes completely. Astonishingly, I could see that I was actually standing at the foot of the mountain. By now I didn't feel terrible. I felt rashy, I felt itchy, I didn't feel great, but my breathing was good, so I was pretty sure that I wasn't going anaphylactic. Unfortunately, I still had no idea what was going on. *[As a side note, once I returned home to Chelmsford, Massachusetts, I was informed that I suffered what is known as"niacin flush". Apparently their high-energy drink is very high in niacin. My being allergic to it (much to my surprise), brought on the reaction; my having consumed a large dose of it greatly intensified this reaction.]*

At that point I had no idea what it was, but I still felt well enough, my muscles were still strong, my wind was good, my spirit was high, and more gifts awaited me, so I decided to make the attempt on the head wall.

The Agony of the Ecstasy

I continued my climb. It was torturous and draining, yet also self-inspiring and truly uplifting, in more ways than one. I could see the ridge ahead that I had eyed from the base of the mountain. This ridge, it seemed, hid behind it Carrantouhill's peak. About three and a half hours later, I hit that ridge. Getting to it was one of the longest short climbs I've ever done in my life. Now I could see Carrantouhill's peak. The successful accomplishing of a first ascent in a flash was to be surpassed only by the final ascent and reaching the summit.

As I ascended up the ridge, the temperature took a sudden and severe drop. Though it was probably somewhere around fifty degrees at Carrantouhill's base, by now and on this ridge, the wind chill had brought temperatures to well-below zero degrees. Everything that I had with me started to ice up. I have some great photos of myself wearing my full gore-tex jacket just covered in ice. I had to put a balaclava on my face and bring up my gore-tex hood because I couldn't have any exposed flesh at this point. The cold, whipping wind combined with the previous rains had deposited hail, about a half inch deep, the size of small marbles all over the rocks. It was like walking on ball bearings.

As I was standing on this ridge, I could see down into Hags Glen, which offered yet another absolutely stunning view. I could also see off in a distance this huge ominous black cloud starting to move in. I was thinking to myself, "Wow, that's not good. If those clouds are precipitous and they come into this area, there's no way I'm going to be able to make it back down that head wall with any kind of inclement weather, especially with the hail and everything else that's already there. I'd be looking at a seriously-impeded descent. "This was really no big deal; at this point, I was already totally soaked from head to toe, so the threat of rain presented no additional cause for concern.

Usually in America, when you climb mountains, they have what are called switchbacks (hair pin turns and inclines that zigzag back and forth), so it's not just straight up like a staircase. In Ireland, there are no switchbacks; there is no zigzag -- you just go straight up the head wall. The incline was good; some of it was hand-over-hand but nothing that required the use of ropes or anything like that. The real problem was, however, that it was all mud and shale which made for very slippery rock and the exposure. Every single step I took had to be so planned out; it had to be so perfect. I knew that, as I got up this head wall with about a thousand feet below me, one wrong move would have me slip on the mud or shale, and I'd go tumbling down. I couldn't allow the thought of a fall resulting in me laying at the bottom of the mountain, through the 'Poo Minefield', five miles in, no cell phone, no walkie-talkie and no help, to enter and linger in my mind. No. I had to stay positively focused.

What was so amazing to me, and I remember this so clearly, is that every once in awhile, at certain points along the way, there would be little breaks of sun that would come through and just illuminate the valley below me. The beautiful palettes of colorful light that illuminated me so at Hags Glen now danced below me; it was another awestruck, breathtaking moment.

Then there were the sheep. Hundreds upon hundreds of sheep dotted these thousand-foot sides of the cliffs along the three sides of the valley. They were everywhere. I simply couldn't imagine how they had made it up to these little perches on the sides of the mountain. I've got amazing photos of them in places I couldn't seem to get to myself.

An Ultimate Test of Courage, Fortitude, and Faith

For what should have been maybe a twenty- or thirty-minute last pitch climb took me close to an hour. I thought coming up the wet shale and the mud earlier in the climb was tough, but going up this last section to the summit was just plain brutal. The below-zero temperatures augmented by the unbearably-strong and persistent wind gusts absolutely required no exposed flesh. Every single step I took was truly another gifted moment of life, considering there was no place for a hold, clear exposure, and the slippery, ball bearings-like hail compromising any form of walking/climbing traction or contact with the rock surface,

I had to break ice off the zippers of my jacket in order to get my gloved hand into the part of my jacket where I stored my water. I had to keep adjusting the water bottles to keep them right next to my body so they wouldn't freeze on me. With the ice removed, I was still having trouble getting the zipper down because the whole thing had frozen up on me. My boot was totally frozen, and my feet were soaking wet. What hadn't yet turned to ice was cold as hell, yet, I just pushed on. What I also had to keep in mind, at this point, was my high metabolism and my available fluid supply. I knew the Lucozade was what I had reacted to, so I had dumped it out. Therefore I had to make this whole last push basically on one quart of water, and I knew that I had to save some for the climb down. I would be worrying about dehydration on top of all this. So I got the weather, a blown out boot, I was soaked and freezing because the wind came up, the black clouds moving in, and night was approaching. It was beautiful.

With each tortuous step, I can remember thinking how I should probably turn around. I kept looking over my shoulder because the black clouds were still out there, and I was thinking that if I don't summit fast and get down faster, I'm going to be sleeping up here over the night. I had enough of the right gear that if I was stuck up here overnight, as long as I didn't go hypothermic or get frostbitten, I would probably make it. But even louder I kept hearing the bed and breakfast woman's words echo in my ears calling her within two hours after my scheduled descent and completion, or else she would be sending out Search and Rescue. There was just no way was I going to put somebody else up here to come and save my butt, so on I pushed.

The Achiever

I received the message. The melody ended. It's just plain *BITTERLY COLD UP THERE!!!!*

I remained up at the peak for no more than maybe one minute, maybe two minutes tops. It was so bitterly cold; I knew that if I stayed up here in the exposed weather conditions like this much longer, I would either go hypothermic or get frostbitten. So as fast as I could, I pulled out my camera, took five photos (one photo in each direction and then one of me with the cross behind me), then started my descent. I distinctly remember watching those huge ominous clouds as they just sort of hovered over a couple of mountains off in the distance. I believe that God protected me when I was on the top and just held the clouds at bay while I started down.

It took me easily an hour to get back down to the first ridge because every step, like I said earlier, was just torturous from the hail. Finally reaching that first ridge, I could see back down in Hag Glen. On this side of the mountain, the sun had started to come out illuminating the wet rock and bringing to life that quiet storm of color and calm all over again. I took a couple of photos and started slowly down. I can remember getting about half way down the headwall, and by this time the sky above me was relatively clear, everything was just glistening with the water and everything that the rain had hit earlier.

I stopped halfway down the headwall. I sat down on a rock, enjoyed the two sandwiches that the bed and breakfast hostess had made me, and drank the last of my water. It felt like the greatest feast that I have ever had in my entire life. With that, I finished up, took a few more photos, and started my final descent.

When I finally got down to the foot of the mountain, I felt a huge sigh of relief, though I still had to make that five-mile trek back to the farm. God is good– all the time. He held back the clouds and saw me safely down. I wondered if it would be too much to ask Him to do something about "POOville" before I got there. It had rained earlier while I was still climbing so I knew that that river crossing at the brook was going to be brutal again. I was, however, able to find a place to cross so I just took a slow walk through the whole thing. I talked to a lot of sheep on the way, asking how they made it up the side of the mountain, a feat that I was still amazed at. I think it's funny how the matter of the "poo" didn't come up until I was way past the sheep, but wading deep through it. The entire climb round trip took about seven hours or so which had me just skirting coming down in the dark by about an hour or so.

Full Circle

I finally made it back to my car and, as promised, knocked on the farm house. The farmer answered and I showed him that it was a good day to climb. He just sort of shook his head and my hand and said, "Well, I'm glad to see you again." We exchanged a few pleasantries and bade each other adieu. I loaded my car, jumped in, and made a bee-line to the nearest pub and the nearest telephone. I ordered the Guinness, called my bed and breakfast lady (I wish I could remember her name), to let her know that I was down. I was healthy, I was good, and I was going to partake in quite a few more Guinness before I headed home. I thought it was well earned.

Mt. Carrantouhill was the most exciting climb I've ever had, and it definitely pushed me to the limits that I never thought were possible. I didn't climb it alone; I had help with this climb. Certainly, I was being watched over, guided, protected and spoken to that day. Perhaps this was a way for me to better appreciate everything all that much more. I certainly learned more about myself and that if you want something that is meant for you to have; you don't give up, just keep going for it.

I was very overwhelmed, yet so very humbled by this experience. Every facet of my life has been forever altered given both the path that GOD had laid for me and the will to walk it with HIS help and guidance. If a person is determined to achieve their goals they can achieve them. It may cost them their health or the threat of their life, but strong will and determination will guide them through the challenge and to the summit of the life's virtual mountain.

Chapter Eleven

Life Is Like Climbing a Mountain. An Exercise for Climbing a Virtual Mountain

The intent behind a literal or figurative mountain climb venture is designed for the climber/explorer to experience a spiritual change. For some adventurers, the experience produces an effect that invariably changes one's self-confidence, fortifies one's self-worth and at minimum; the experience places a lens for a different view on one's horizon.

The purpose of the following exercise is to present a strategic working plan to ensure and encourage positive personal or organizational transformation. The exercise, when completed, is guaranteed to produce an opportunity for the reader/adventurer to consider a new attitude and perspective about life and its many challenges. The exercise will certainly introduce realities that parallel a literal mountain climb, but these are presented within a figurative or virtual mountain climb framework. Some aspects of change for individuals or organizations to be realized include, but are not limited to, attitude, methodology or approach to performing particular functions, and capacity building.

This exercise will essentially provide a road map for the explorer to follow, as a sure plan to succeed at identifying, defining, and then climbing a virtual mountain or a series of mountains that are inherently implanted within the physical and spiritual experience we call life.

The questions are personalized to the reader/explorer (fill in the blanks):

Questions/Tasks

#1. What is your mountain?
     For example: Buy a house, get married, etc.

_____

#2. Be flexible.

#3. Is there more than one mountain you would like to climb? If
     so, list and when?

     _____

     _____

     _____

#4. Should any of the other mountains that you would like to
     climb take priority over the first mountain that you listed? If
     so, list and when?
     For example, purchase a vehicle in three months.

     _____

     _____

     _____

#5. Define your mission to climb this particular mountain
For example:
   a. What is the makeup or characteristics or details about this particular mountain?
   b. Why do you want to climb this particular mountain?
   c. How do you plan to climb this particular mountain?
   d. Where is this particular mountain?
   e. When would you like to climb this particular mountain?
   f. With whom do you plan to climb this particular mountain?

#6. How big is your mountain?

#7. What is your capacity to climb this particular mountain?

#8. How is your health?

#9. How is your wealth?

#10. How important is it to you to climb this particular mountain?

#11. When do you want to climb this particular mountain? How soon?

#12. Will you plan to climb this particular mountain alone?

#13. Will someone else climb with you? If yes, how well do you know this person(s)?

#14. Are you determined to make this climb if the plans to climb with others do not work out?

#15. Investigate the current status of this particular mountain.

#16. Investigate the history behind this particular mountain.

#17. Investigate the future trends of this particular mountain.

#18.   Investigate this particular mountain to understand what tools and skills are needed for a successful climb experience.

#19.   Devise a back up plan for this particular mountain climb.

#20.   **Gear up... and Go!**

About the Author

According to many accounts, James Edward Bruce, Sr., Ph.D. is a renaissance man. He is multi-talented, multi-skilled, multi-national, multi-lingual, multi-faceted and multi-tasking. He is a man that wears many hats and has many "irons in the fire", yet is very accomplished. Mr. Bruce is focused and determined to inform, educate, inspire, and motivate people throughout the world to explore their virtual mountains and to reach the peak of whatever level they aspire.

James Bruce, Sr. recently pursued a Ph.D. in Organization Management from the School of Business and Technology at Capella University in Minneapolis, Minnesota. As an entrepreneur for almost 25 years, and now a Business Consultant and Motivational Expert, he travels throughout the United States and abroad to motivate and stimulate individuals, groups and organizations toward developing a strategic plan for positive change.

James' international travel experiences to more than 60 countries have gifted him with an innocent or natural love for people and their life testimonials. At least two common themes that emerged

DR. JAMES E. BRUCE

from meeting so many people worldwide have been that, (1) all people can identify with physical mountains, and (2) all people have personal goals, dreams and aspirations, although articulating them might sometimes be a challenge. James posits that some people simply need to be informed of their life options. Some explorers need to be inspired and motivated to become believers and achievers.

His universal travels have seasoned his understanding for how to guide individuals, groups, and organizations toward accomplishing a virtual climb that might take the form of a realized goal, dream or aspiration. A successful virtual mountain climb is only possible with the use of the appropriate tool. James is confident that this book, "Life is like climbing a mountain", is that tool.

Thoughts

LIFE IS LIKE CLIMBING A MOUNTAIN

The objective of this book is to inform, educate, inspire, and motivate individuals and groups toward understanding oneself and others through a literal or virtual mountain climbing experience. The aim is to introduce the reader to a literary journey that involves the process and the act of mountain climbing. This book brings forth the recognition that, just as literal mountains may be comprised of rocks, trees, ice, snow, and dirt, either singularly or in any combination, so, too, are we, as individuals, comprised of differing traits, strengths, values, mores, and beliefs that offer both specific strengths and weaknesses that alternate given the environment that surround us, the situation presented to us and what we feel within us. A volcanic mountain, it should be noted, is more representative to one's inner self. Similar to that of this 'living rock', changes occur subtly, deep within us, sometimes immediate and many times occurring unnoticed by us over long periods of time. Like the sudden sight of smoke or vibrations felt from underground, it is only during the external expression of change do we realize that we, and those around us, are merely experiencing the change that has long since occurred. The inherent volatility of this 'living rock' parallels the vulnerability, potential explosiveness, and yet the total dependencies that exist in the individual human experience, as well as within our local and world communities.

These physical mountains are used as a metaphor to offer insight into understanding the dynamics and challenges that are involved in the process of climbing a virtual mountain. The mountain climbing process might become more meaningful to an explorer who climbs a virtual mountain that may ultimately take the form of realizing a goal, dream, or aspiration. This book explores the spiritual aspect of the physical mountain, particularly how the physical mountain has been a reference place for some people whose successful climb offer testimony to a life-changing experience.

This mountain climbing model is useful towards attaining individual, personal or collective goals, set in areas such as education, business, wealth building, job or career development, marriage, political aspirations, geographical relocating, re-establishing oneself, raising children, leading or managing sports teams, hiring and managing a work force, or even military strategy. This "climbing a mountain model" can be used for creating a strategic map towards achieving other personal goals, such as writing a book, building a house from the ground up, or regaining physical or mental health. Similarly, for organizations, this "climbing a mountain model" can be used as a guide when setting an organization's growth plans in motion. The principles are the same.

Finally, this book provides a strategic working roadmap that will transform the reader to an explorer, to a believer, and finally, to an achiever. The achiever in retrospect will be inspired to recall and then recite the most powerful words: *I said I can*, *I know that I would*, and *I made it happen*.
–James E. Bruce, Sr., Ph.D.